CHOPPED

"...what a delightful kosher companion to *Chicken Soup*."

—Jerry Cutler, Rabbi, Creative Arts Temple,
author of *The Celebrity Kosher Cookbook*

"...any way you serve it, it's downright delectable—
a gourmet literary treat!"

—Robert Kotler, M.D., author of
Secrets of a Beverly Hills Cosmetic Surgeon

"...has all the vital nutrients for a healthy best-seller."

—Earl Mindell, Ph.D., author of
The Vitamin Bible

"...filled with heartwarming stories that bring out the *best* of the human spirit."

—Rosalene Glickman, Ph.D.,
author of *Optimal Thinking*

"...one of the interesting things about reading these stories is that I personally know some of the contributing authors. You'll soon discover what a sound investment you've made in this inspiring book."

—Marvin Marshall, author of *Discipline without Stress® Punishments, or Rewards* and *Fostering Social Responsibility*

"...every story is heartwarming and right on target with all winning ingredients for success."

—Ivan Burnell, author of *The Road to a Happier Marriage*

"...if someone's not moved by at least one of these stories, then their heart must be made of stone."

—Rennie Gabriel, author of *Wealth On Any Income*

"...what good company these literary voices are!"

—Gloria Delaney, author of *Other Voices, Other Faces*

"...you don't have to be Jewish to love *this* chopped liver."

—Paul Westfall, editor/publisher of *In!Magazine*

"...people all over the world would enjoy this anthology—it's got that international flavor."

—Louisa Moritz, actress/author of *Reborn*

"...this could be the start if something big!"

—Mary Jane Popp, host, KTKZ Radio, Sacramento

"...I give this unforgetable opus a 3-M rating—marvelous, monumental & memorable!"

—Arthur Bornstein, author of
Memory Course Training

"...I could kick myself for not getting in on the first edition—you can bet I'll submit a story for the next serving."

—Peggi Ridgway, author of
Web Savvy for Small Business

"...oo, la, la! This chopped liver is as appetizing as the pate de foie in my French native land, New Caladonia. Bon appetit!"

—Georgette O'Connor, author of *Fidelity on Trial*

"... I couldn't get enough of these tasty morsels!"

—Rich De Leo, talk host, WFBG Radio, Altoona, PA

"...even in the heartland of America where I am, everyone's eating up this chopped liver!"

—Jerry Puffer, host, KSEN Radio, Shelby, MT

"...I never leave home without it...this book is my buddy on all trips."
—Willy Southall, author of *Hyssop: Superior Healing Power*

"...offers more love and healing than Mom's home cooking!"

—Susan Allan, author of *Divorce: The Marry-Go-Round*

"...I've been in the culinary PR biz for over 50 years—it's about time someone finally concocted this award-winning concept."
—Leo Pearlstein, author of *Celebrity Stew*

"...not to worry—our relatives will buy enough copies now that our mom, Devra Hill, is included in this diversified collection."

—Judi & Shari Zucker, co-authors of *Double Your Energy With Half the Effort*

Chopped Liver
for the American Spirit

*To Ronald,
All the very
best!
Rick Searfoss*

CHOPPED LIVER FOR THE AMERICAN SPIRIT

To Sarah,
Mazel tov!
Best,
Lily Barber

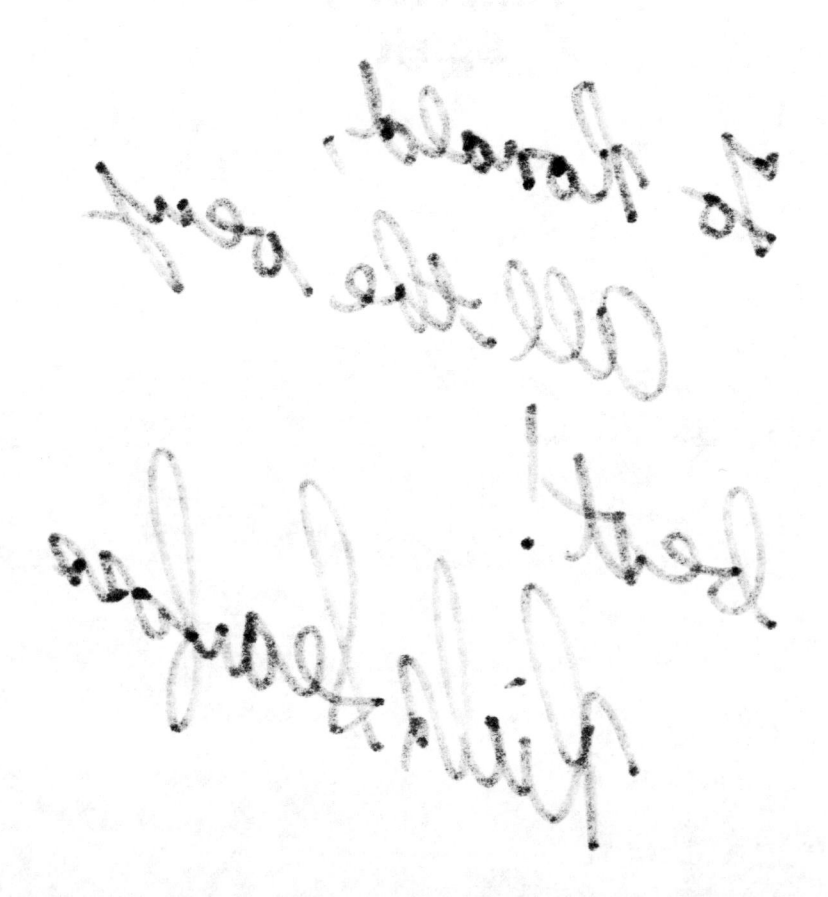

Chopped Liver
for the American Spirit

52 stories of people overcoming difficult and frustrating circumstances and turning them into something meaningful, productive and fulfilling.

Ernie Weckbaugh

Best-Seller Books

© 2003 by Best-Seller Books

All rights reserved. No part of the publication may be reproduced, stored in a retrieval system, or transmitted, in any form or by means electronic, mechanical or by photocopying, recording or otherwise, except for the inclusion of brief quotation from a review, without prior permission in writing from the author.

10 9 8 7 6 5 4 3 2 1

ISBN 1-881474-45-3
Library of Congress Catalog Card Number 2003106352

Published by Best-Seller Books and Casa Graphics, Inc., Burbank, California • casag@wgn.net

Book layout, cover design, and illustrations by Ernie Weckbaugh of Casa Graphics, Inc., Burbank, CA.

Manufactured in the United States of America by KNI, Inc. of Anaheim, California, and Sir Speedy® of Whittier, California.

Dedication

This book is dedicated to the spirit of "chopped liver," and to all our talented authors who shared their stories. They took chopped liver situations in their lives, or in the life of someone close to them and, with imagination, courage and love, turned a difficult, sometimes frustrating circumstance into something meaningful, productive and fulfilling.

Chopped Liver and *the American Spirit* seem to go hand-in-hand. Where else but in a country full of freedom and free spirits do you see such enterprise, such can-do attitudes, where anything can and does happen—including the miraculous?

The following page says in verse what we owe to this feeling. We can and will overcome, a concept central to the civil rights movement that began in the '50s. When our personal rights, freedoms and privileges are challenged, we as Americans are famous for taking a mess and turning it into an achievement.

Owed to Chopped Liver

If chopped liver to you is a mystery,
Then misfortune is not in your history.
If you feel like a winner
And take friends out to dinner,
No one there, I'll bet, orders chopped liver.

When the bill comes to you, you say, "*How much* ?!?!"
It's too late to suggest that they "go dutch."
They're all fat from their dinner
But you're feeling much thinner.
All *you're* able to eat is chopped liver.

I'm been thinking of buying a sports car...
A Mercedes, a Lexus, a Jaguar.
But all *I* can afford
Is a Focus from Ford . . .
On its vanity plate—CHOP LVR.

A friend of mine's late uncle Mo,
Who had nothing, *but nothing,* but dough.
When his will is recited—
Just his children divide it.
His nephew says, "What—I'm chopped liver?"

Opportunity comes like a feast
Where filet mignon is the *least*.
And it goes to the one
Who can get the job done,
And the rest can *"feast"* on chopped liver.

—*Ernie Weckbaugh*

Introduction

Successful people solve *problems every day,*
whereas failures create *problems on a daily basis.*

The stories in this book prove that "chopped liver" is not the end, but can be a beginning of great things in your life. Looking back on a century of greed and violence, the world hungers for the emergence of a kinder millennium. In *Chopped Liver for the American Spirit*, a mirror reflects tiny bits of light and hope from the past giving us the courage and confidence to turn and face forward. It shows that one person or event can often make an amazing difference in the lives of others.

The popular term "chopped liver" is a joke among gourmet appetites—the least among the best. It's symbolic of situations that can't get any worse, yet can be the starting point of personal triumph.

The recurring theme is a like rope dangling over the cliff to an accident victim. It is the offer we can't refuse—that single act we can't do for ourselves, the offer of a hand instead of a fist, or the rare quality of listening and understanding instead of harsh condemnation in a world of hurt.

This book helps us explore the attic of our mind. The ideas we take in stimulate the ones that exist. This can be an inspiring synthesis of thought, combining those concepts we often ponder, discuss and treasure.

Humans live from insight to insight. From birth our life is a continuous stream of revelations. The longer they are integrated into and throughout our adult lives, the happier we remain. Anxiety in our lives is a measure of our own limitations.

As you read the stories in *Chopped Liver*, let your mind be an actor. Take the part of each contributing author as if you were cast to play the leading role in their story. Involve yourself as a character who's learning a part and projecting his persona onto the written word, or might try to see the scenario through the eyes of the playwright.

This book is an experiment in multiple creativity. It has been a chance to tap into a society of doers, people who make things happen, whose "luck" results from a lot of effort. They are above the ordinary in being able to observe life around them and to use it for inspiration. Let their inspiration become yours.

—*Ernie Weckbaugh*

Table of

Dan Poynter	Foreword	9
1-**John H. Dilkes**	A Tribute (to A. P. Giannini)	11
2-**Margaret Schumacher**	A Man of Vision	15
3-**Mariann Aalda**	Christopher's Wisdom	19
4-**Dr. Walter Hofmann**	A Little Boy	25
5-**Lisa Todd**	Tall Tale Winner	31
6-**Val Middlebrook**	Angels on the Highway	35
7-**Bernice Schachter**	Artist at Work	41
8-**James F. Holt**	Huckleberry Holt	47
9-**Joyce Spizer**	Goodbye Eye	53
10-**Ellen Reid**	The Meaning of Life Is Dinner	59
11-**Dr. Michael Fenlon**	The Bridge Builder	63
12-**Beverly Bacon**	Looking Forward to 30	69
13-**Wink Martindale**	The Night Music Changed	73
14-**Lael Littke**	Diamonds In My Backyard	77
15-**Dr. Gene Manusov**	A Red Marble	83
16-**Dr. Bob West**	West's Point	87
17-**Dr. Roger Leir**	Alone In the Universe	93
18-**John Alston**	Lessons In a Legacy	99
19-**Dr. Rex Ingraham**	A Gift of Trust	105
20-**Ernest Lewis Weckbaugh**	Bombs Bursting In Air	109
21-**Dr. Gray & Joanne Berg**	From "The Wall" to "Ground Zero"	113
22-**Janie Lee**	Of Horses and Bathtubs	119
23-**Dottie Walters**	Opportunity Is Always "At Hand"	123
24-**Patty Palmer Weckbaugh**	The Murder Mystery that Killed the Audience	131
25-**Elizabeth Thompson**	The Character Man	135
26-**Tad Callister**	A Tower of Generosity	139

Contents

27-	**Glenn Ackerman**	Invisibility & Fame	143
28-	**Rick Searfoss** (Astronaut Commander)	From Cold War Warrior Opponents to Space Explorer Colleagues	149
29-	**Dr. Harris Done**	Ambassadors of Good Teeth	155
30-	**Ernie & Patty Weckbaugh**	Woman's Place Is In the House... or the Senate!	159
31-	**Patty Weckbaugh**	It's *Her* Business	163
32-	**Ray Schnieders**	No Mountain Too High	167
33-	**Ernie Weckbaugh**	Against *All* Odds	175
34-	**Ed Hibler**	Sex, Sin, and Satisfaction in the Classroom	179
35-	**Pilar McRae**	A Tree Grows In El Monte	185
36-	**John Ernst**	Dumb-Duh-Dumb-Dumb	189
37-	**Dr. Ed & Jackie Hibler**	Oh, Those Gutsy Geezers!	195
38-	**Judith I. (Chase) Jefferies**	"Go For It"	201
39-	**Bill Derringer**	My Bubba's Weekly Meeting	207
40-	**Esther Pearlman**	My Bodyguard	213
41-	**Frank Becker**	The Music Man of Japan	219
42-	**Dr. William Dahlberg**	A Legend In His Time	223
43-	**Bernadene Coleman**	Letting Go	227
44-	**Margaret Rector**	The Evening Purse	235
45-	**Don Albrecht**	Gold Fever	239
46-	**Susan Moss**	Cancer Saved My Life	243
47-	**Sol Marshall**	The Keys to My Success	249
48-	**Victoria Bullis**	Hong Kong Blues	253
49-	**Dr. Devra Hill**	Wild, Wild West!	261
50-	**Dr. Audrey Reed**	Snapshots	265
51-	**Patricia Rust**	Not Even a Bullet In His Head Could Stop Him	269
52-	**Mariann Aalda**	Team Momma	275

Foreword

This book is really "the cat's meow!"

I have always felt authors should seek out and target new, untapped audiences. Sometimes it's right under their noses—a ready-made following.

Such was the good fortune of Book Publicists of Southern California with the undertaking of this literary endeavor. Of the close to 1,000 BPSC members, few are full-time working PR folk; most are writers/authors/reporters, all publicists "at heart," with a strong passion for the written word.

Dan Poynter

So when Irwin Zucker, the founder/president emeritus of this glorious organization, came up with the concept of *Chopped Liver for the American Spirit*—a take off on the highly successful *Chicken Soup for the Soul* series—there was much rejoicing in the ranks of BPSC, envisioning a readership of at least 1,000.

BPSC president Ernie Weckbaugh and his club v-p, wife Patty were enthusiastic over the project. They quickly sought out authors both in and out of the BPSC group to pen a chapter dealing with the theme "one day you're chopped liver...the next filet mignon."

The result is this dazzling collection of stories of everlasting interest (thank you, *Reader's Digest*)—heartwarming, humorous, nostalgic, and inspirational, with unpredictable twists and surprises. Credit the Weckbaughs and BPSC members Lael Littke and Judith Jefferies for heading up the editorial board for this terrific tome.

An interesting sidelight—one of the first entries was a chapter by John Dilkes, a sprightly 92, who came to the U.S. from England some 20 years ago. He encouraged his British-born daughter, Margaret Schumacher and her American hubby, David, the noted real estate author, to also contribute a chapter that captures the American spirit.

As the author of *The Older Cat* (among some 100-plus books I've written), I can say I've thoroughly enjoyed each of the chapters. I've often treated cats I have cared for and loved to plates of chopped liver—which is why I rate this book *the cat's meow!*

Have a purr-fectly wonderful time with it!

—Dan Poynter, author of *The Self-Publishing Manual*

JOHN H. DILKES

President of the Canterbury Retirement Home, Rancho Palos Verdes, John came to California in 1982. He left school at 14 to work in a textile factory at its lowest ladder for just over one penny per hour. After army service he became a Chartered Surveyor and Valuation Officer for Inland Revenue, Newark, England.

He has crossed the Atlantic on the Oriana, flown on the Concord, and has enjoyed worldwide cruises. He has been a ballroom dancer, poet, and has painted 25 pictures in the last two years. He appeared as Fred Astaire at a local theatre on February 2003 at the age of 91.

Phone: 310-541-7262 / Fax: 310-379-9710

1 A Tribute

*to A.P. Giannini,
Founder of Bank of America
by John H. Dilkes*

A wonderful man, born the sixth of May
In 1870, a century away.
He was A.P. and a friend to all,
Enjoyed helping people whatever their call.

In his early years he worked hard and more
At his pa's busy fruit and produce store.
His contracts with farmers were always fair.
For his customers A.P. was always there.

At just thirty-four, elected board member
Of a Bay area bank, this brand new "ember"
"Flared up" as they all paid heed to the rich,
Then quickly decided to change his "pitch."

So he set up the Bank of Italy that year.
A.P. and the vision of his staff was clear.
He explained what a bank could do for all,
And welcomed the poor when they came to call.

1906, San Francisco's distress,
The fire-damage toll was a terrible mess.
An out-of-door cash desk, devoid of swank,
With only two barrels and a wooden plank.

A.P. knew many who needed help.
He arranged small loans without a yelp.
Trusting their character, he had his reward,
Causing thousands of new friends to come aboard.

The earthquake in '06 transformed his life,
He found that banking could ease other's strife.
In his life's ambition to fulfill his mission,
A system of branches came to fruition.

Building California became his aim,
Loans to fruit, vegetable, wine trades won him fame.
He was always careful to arrange a good deal,
And satisfy customers without a squeal.

1930 with 300 branches to his dream
A.P. changed the name to Bank of America—*supreme!*
This new bank bought regional bonds by the billions,
Creating new jobs for millions and millions.

When the Golden Gate Bridge began that spring
Of '33, municipal bonds were the thing
That made it possible from B of A.
Later Hollywood, Disneyland—he saved the day.

Each year Bank Americans, on a special date,
Pay honor to "A.P." and celebrate
His richness of spirit. This boy in his prime
Left footprints behind in the sands of time.

John H. Dilkes

DR. DAVID and MARGARET SCHUMACHER

David T. Schumacher, Ph.D., CCIM, is the author of *Buy and Hold Real Estate Strategy* (John Wiley & Sons, 1992). He has personally appraised over 3,000 properties including several Las Vegas Hotels, multiple interests on Santa Catalina Island and estates owned by Bob Hope, Zsa Zsa Gabor, Marion Davies and Mary Mannering.

He is the author of textbooks on appraising and investment building and he has taught advanced real estate appraisal courses for the Calif. Department of Real Estate, Los Angeles City College and UCLA Extension. He retired in 1990 and currently writes monthly articles for *Creative Real Estate Magazine*. His current book is *Buy & Hold, 7 Steps to a Real Estate Fortune*, also available in audio format abridged, was selected as one of the best real estate books by Robert Bruss, Nationally Syndicated Real Estate Columnist. It received an IRWIN Award from the Book Publicists of Southern California and the Pinnacle Achievement Award for best book in the business category from NABE (North American Bookdealers Exchange), Oregon.

Dr. and Mrs. David Schumacher donated $1 million in 1999 to the City of Hermosa Beach, California for the renovation of the Schumacher Pier Plaza in memory of David's identical twin brother, Paul William Schumacher.

2 A Man of Vision

by David Schumacher, Ph.D., and Margaret Schumacher

On a bright summer day in August of 1919, two adorable identical twin boys, David and Paul Schumacher, were born in downtown Los Angeles, California. They were perfect in body and soul except for their eyes, which were defective from the genetically inherited disease called progressive myopia. This was to haunt them for the rest of their lives. They struggled in school to read the blackboard. Both boys wore thick glasses which the other children ridiculed. But in spite of the mockery, they had the consolation of each other's company.

They enjoyed playing together and had doting parents in an always loving, warm family atmosphere. Their parents, Max and Minnie, gave them a solid moral upbringing and encouraged them from their youth to invest in real estate instead of frivolous items. When they wanted a car, their mother suggested they invest their savings in a small house. She told them the house would bring in more than enough return to have the car they were anxious to purchase. How wise Minnie was.

Imagine the struggle to obtain a driver's license, especially so as the years passed by. David attempted to memorize the vision chart in his desperation to drive. All his life David has avoided being reliant on other people to assist him until the last few years, when he lost his sight completely.

Max and Minnie sent them to a special school, but the boys could not join in the usual sporting activities. They were faced with many restrictions, but always remained positive in their outlook on life. They were able to gain sufficient education to proceed to college and, later in life, David received a Ph.D. His father Max owned a dairy and creamery, so David went to the University of California at Davis to study agriculture.

David's love of ice cream almost cost the company all the profits. His cousin Marvin would serve in the creamery, and just as David reached out to take the proffered cone, Marvin would let it drop to the floor. This was among the simple boyish tricks they used to play on each other in those days. Being identical twins, David and Paul got a kick out of playing pranks on friends and visitors since it was almost impossible to tell them apart.

At 40 years of age, David lost all of his money in the commodities market. It was a devastating blow. He figured he knew more about real estate than the future of peas, beans and corn, and he quickly moved into the real estate field to become a very successful appraiser. Paul did likewise. They both worked hard and played hard. David appraised the Los Angeles "Follies" (the costume collection, not the glamorous show girls inside the fancy garments). He appraised properties on Catalina Island, spending three months there, and appraised many of the casinos and hotels in Las Vegas.

Paul passed away at the early age of 51. David struggled through the grief and carefully planned the course of his life knowing full well he might be legally blind one day. In his spare time, David traveled extensively around the world as both a tourist and a tour leader. He reveled in unusual situations as his way of getting thrills. He delighted in having a huge snake draped around his neck in Bangkok.

In Lagos, Nigeria, a peddler threw a big black spider onto David's head when he refused to purchase a second carved statue. Everyone screamed as the spider crawled down David's neck. He hastily knocked the creature to the ground, but the incident could have had deadly consequences.

In Papua, New Guinea, he bravely put his hands in the water to feel baby crocodiles swimming beside their canoe on the Sepik River.

David worried about getting married, and was deeply concerned about producing children who might lose their sight. It was on one of his many cruises that we met. I was 25 years younger, born in Robin Hood's territory in England. Ironically, it was love at first sight since David saw reasonably well back then. We were married in England in 1977, but the first major setback occurred when David suffered a detached retina three months after our wedding. Surgically repaired, the retina detached again later, and he lost the sight of his left eye completely. I stood by him through it all. Here I was in a strange new environment, sustained only by my love for David. I knew our circumstances could be reversed and that we could weather this storm together.

His continued eye problems could not deter our desire for travel and adventure. David and I were among the first American tourist groups to journey to China and Mongolia in 1979. We survived a monstrous hurricane on the Fiji Islands, and spent the night in a bus that listed at a 45-degree angle in mud surrounded by torrents of swirling water. This was near the Ross River, outside Alice Springs, Australia.

Throughout our married life, David and I have spent less than six months apart. We have communicated well and have learned to exchange our life's roles. First David was the decision maker, then, when his sight diminished, I took over as the dominant one. In this marriage of great learning, David has taught me many vital lessons regarding the real estate business with its multiple facets, and how to promote his book on real estate, *Buy and Hold, 7 Steps to a Real Estate Fortune.*

We have learned to adapt to living with legal blindness. Suddenly everything at home had to be in its proper place all the time to avoid accidents. Trips away from home had to involve accommodations for the handicapped for safety and comfort. People with a severe handicap want to be treated like normal people, and David would like people not to know, but it's difficult trying to lead a normal life when you're unable to see.

His greatest contribution was to write the book after he lost his sight so he could share his real estate knowledge and the method by which he acquired his wealth. Not a day passes that he is not an inspiration to our friends and me. He revels in helping people with their real estate problems, receiving numerous phone calls on a daily basis. David yearns to give back a few of the great rewards he's received while he is still of strong mind and body. He recently made an outstanding recovery from a stroke. His life has been a story of a man of many dreams and goals, most of which he's made happen through persistence and a great zest for life.

MARIANN AALDA, C.Ht., and CHRISTOPHER HARRISON

3 Christopher's Wisdom
by Mariann Aalda

Angie died.

For the first four years of my life, my cousin Angie had been the saving grace of my childhood. Her family and mine shared a two-flat building on the South Side of Chicago. When she was a teenager, I was her toddler sidekick, entertaining her and her friends by making up little songs and dances and mimicking the popular television performers of the day.

Angie championed my youthful longings to become an actress and, when she graduated from college and started teaching, she paid for my classes in ballet, piano and drama in a performing arts program for children at Chicago's Roosevelt University. She never missed a performance and never failed to tell me how "dazzlingly, wonderfully brilliant" I was when it was over.

She was the first person in my life that I can remember who truly made me feel special. I was determined that when I grew up I would validate her belief in me. I only wish she'd lived to see it.

But in the time it takes to say "God, help me, I just can't take it any more," she was gone...just like that. Kaput. Finito. Asked and answered...outta here. Dead at 43 from a brain aneurysm. Putting everyone else ahead of herself, Angie had started to experience depression in a way that she'd felt offered no solutions. In an odd, cosmic "be careful what you ask for" kind of way, I guess she found one.

It was four forty-five in the morning when I got "the call." I was now an adult, living in New York, and wavering about whether to continue to pursue an elusive acting career or get a "real" job. Angie was living in Arizona.

Upon hearing the news, I instinctively slipped my arm out of one of the sleeves of my bathrobe to muffle my sobs with it. It was a habit I'd acquired early in life when my parents bought a home in the suburbs and ripped me away from my cousins, Angie and her younger sister, Joanie.

Wiping the sleep out of his eyes, my son Christopher shuffled into the living room in his powder-blue jumpsuit pajamas with the yellow satin bunny rabbit running down the right side and the white plastic feet that were all crackled from far too-numerous washings. He stopped in front of me and stood very still, waiting. He had just turned four years old.

Eventually, I stopped crying long enough for him to ask, "What's the matter, mommy?"

My sadness was now infused with dread. How does one explain death to a four-year old? I proceeded carefully.

"Remember Cousin Angie?"

He nodded.

"Remember when she came to visit us with the kids last summer and we all had such a good time?"

He nodded again.

"Well, she...she's..." I helplessly groped for the right words... none came. "She's gone."

"She's gone?"

I nodded.

"Where did she go?"

By now, my heart was beating out of my chest like a tom-tom. I wasn't ready for this...

"She's...she's up in...Heaven.

"See, Heaven is the place you go to when you...die. Everybody goes there eventually, so it's not a *bad* thing, it's just that...I know I won't get to see Angie again until I get there, and...that probably won't be for a very, very long time and...and...I'm really, really going to miss her." I prayed that my clumsy explanation would satisfy him. I held my breath.

Christopher stared at me with those big dark eyes of his that, because of the way they were being illumined by the light of the dawning sun, suddenly looked like two sparkling chunks of glinting black coal.

Slowly he walked over to me and gently placed his left hand on top of my right one, which I had unconsciously been clenching into a tight fist.

"Don't cry, mommy." he said softly.

"You have to die so that you can live, because if you didn't die, you wouldn't live."

And then, like a little Buddha, he turned and walked — not shuffling this time — back to his room and went to sleep.

Obviously, Christopher was aware of something that I had long forgotten. His little hands were electric when they touched mine and goosebumps immediately spread all over my body. In fact they still do, whenever I tell this story.

It was as though Christopher had channeled some powerfully commanding life-force, some great "Wisdom of the Ages" the profoundness of which was exceeded only by its simplicity.

*Could this have been **God** talking through him?*

In any case, it had that effect. Christopher's words jolted me into questioning what had to die in *my* life so that *I* could truly live. Unlike Angie, I wasn't ready for *eternal* life yet, so I knew I had to make some changes in this one.

Getting into therapy was the first change. Learning how to say "No" was the second, and deciding to seriously pursue my dreams for an acting career despite overwhelming admonitions of the "foolishness" of it, was the third. Since this is not a spill-your-guts-and-tell-all tome, I won't enumerate the rest of them, but be assured that there were many. I handled them all by following the "How do you eat an elephant?" Method – one bite at a time. And four years later I was starring in the ABC soap opera *Edge of Night* as the feisty young attorney, DiDi Bannister. So much for foolishness.

And now, I suggest to you that whatever it is in *your* life that you *just can't take any more,* GET RID OF IT or it will kill you. Or maybe even worse it will kill your *spirit*. And what could be worse than coming to the end of your physical life with the realization that you never really lived it...at least not in the way you had once aspired to. So "die" to all the negative thoughts, negative circumstances and negative people in your life and...

SING YOUR SONG! DANCE YOUR DANCE!

TELL YOUR STORY! FLY YOUR KITE!

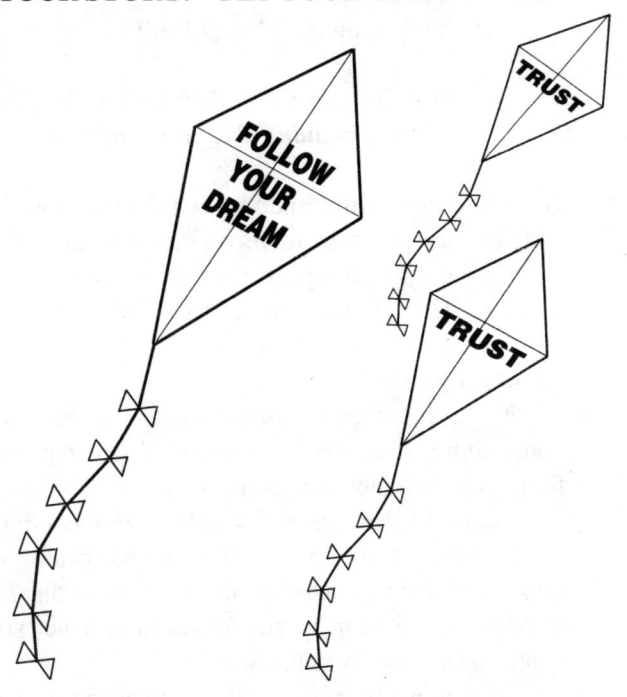

Celebrate your life as the *gift* that it is. Surround yourself with kindred souls who will only love and support your joy in doing so. Give encouragement to someone in your life in the way that Angie did for me...but remember also to give that same encouragement to yourself.

Trust yourself. Trust in your dreams. Trust that when you're willing to let go of something, something else of greater stature, grander proportions and higher fulfillment always moves in to replace it. Die to the *darkness* and embrace the *light*. Trust that in every ending lies the seeds of a new beginning. Trust that even physical death is merely a threshold to the *eternal* life of the soul.

One more thing...remember to *really* listen to your children. They come to us bearing wisdom we may have long forgotten.

And, oh yeah, from time to time, remind them of how dazzlingly, wonderfully brilliant they are...and trust that you are, too.

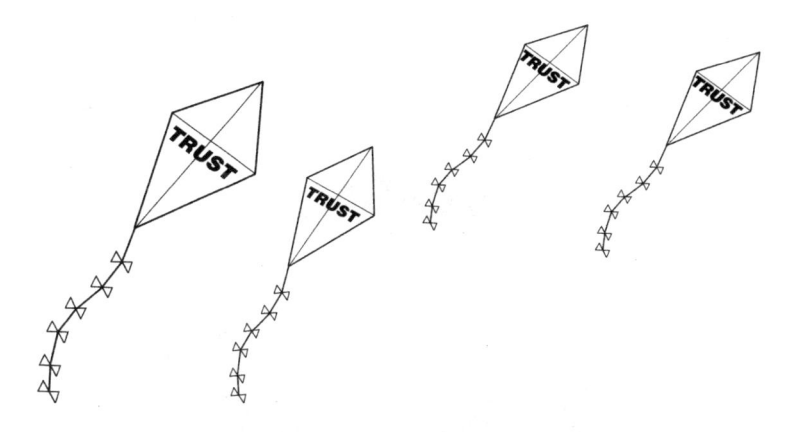

This story is from *My Kid Is My Guru, 21 Days to Uncast the Spell of Negative Beliefs and Live the Life of Your Dreams*, an audio and self-help workbook series which engages the Ericksonian Hypnosis model of storytelling. The first in the series will be available in the summer of 2003.

In addition to *Edge of Night*, highlights of Mariann's twenty-plus-year acting career include co-starring in the films *Class Act* and *Nobody's Perfect*; series regular roles on the CBS sitcom *The Royal Family* and HBO's *First & Ten*; recurring roles on *Sunset Beach* on NBC, *Designing Women* (as Anthony's notorious yuppy-from-hell girlfriend, Lita Ford), and co-hosting the lifestyle magazine show, *Designs for Living* for the USA Network. As a certified clinical hypnotherapist, she also incorporates motivational speaking, workshops and volunteer work into her acting and writing schedules and was named "Volunteer of the Year" by the Los Angeles Dept. of Children's Services for her work with disadvantaged youth.

Christopher Harrison has more than fulfilled the wisdom he displayed as a little boy. He is a graduate of the prestigious Rochester Institute of Technology in Rochester, N.Y., and works for Cisco Systems in San Jose, CA, as an electrical engineer and technical marketing specialist. He is also involved in outreach programs for young people through the National Society of Black Engineers (NSBE).

They both can be reached at www.aaldaanswers.com.

DR. WALTER DAVID HOFMANN

Dr. Hofmann is now retired and living in La Jolla, California. He remains active as a columnist for several newspapers answering questions related to his life experiences. He is on the volunteer psychiatric faculty at U.C.S.D. and on the Crisis Team of the San Diego Police Department. You can contact him at: DrDavidLaJolla@aol.com.

4 A Little Boy
by Walter David Hofmann, M.D.

Her hair was bright red. Her name was Avis Horton. To the little boy it seemed a strange name. She was his fifth grade teacher and he enjoyed learning things in this new world. He felt very lucky. Although he had been born in America, his parents had emigrated from Central Europe and he was glad to be in school in a country that seemed to be friendlier than the one his parents talked about.

He was eleven years old. Short. Freckled face. Barefoot, as were most of the rest of the kids in this two-room schoolhouse in this small farm community in central California.

He says that he remembers it very clearly. His teacher had pulled up a chair close to his desk and was holding his left hand with both of hers. "You will go on to school and do many worthwhile things." The little boy wondered what she meant. She said, "You will work hard; you will help many others." He did not know what she was talking about. It seemed to him that he knew very little about what was going on around him. He knew nothing about the future.

His family called him *der kleine Perfessor*. It was neither a compliment nor a criticism. They saw in him a desire to study and to learn, and to help others to learn. Having arrived from southern Germany just twelve years before, the family spoke only German around the house. His mother had given him the title of the little professor because he seemed so eager to help her learn the English language. His mother had many duties around the house caring for her large family. She had found it a welcome relief to listen to the radio to several daily soap operas as she was washing the morning stack of dishes. Many days when he returned home from school, she plied him with questions and more questions. She would ask, "Walder, wie heist es wen man sagt, 'I am jealous'?" She waited expectantly for a simple answer. On the radio that day the word "jealous" had been used and she had no idea what it meant. The little boy often knew the answers to the questions that his mother asked him, but this one stumped him. He would ask his red-haired teacher in school the next day and find out.

Maybe that is why Mrs. Horton held his hand so tenderly. She was not given to prophetic statements. She seemed to see in him a desire to learn and was giving him some words of encouragement.

The little boy was the fifth child in a family of eight. He had four older siblings who were born in Germany. There were two older brothers and an older sister. One brother was just one year older than he was. That brother had come over on the boat as a newborn infant. The little boy had three younger siblings. Another brother and two more sisters. The grandparents had arrived two years earlier from a country struggling with economic and social unrest. America was the land of opportunity. Having paved the way, the grandparents had bought a small farm and had called for the rest of the family to join them. The parents bundled up the four kids and made the boat trip across the ocean and the train trip across the new country.

This little boy felt richly blessed. He knew little of the world outside his small village of German immigrant farmers. Some folks said that the town of Valley Home had 241 people. But to him it seemed like a big family. On Sunday afternoons he spent endless hours playing with his brothers and sisters, or with the many neighbors who would often drop by to join in the fun. Most of them were of Germanic origin, but some were Black and some were from Mexico. Sometimes he got so tired from playing all the running games that he had to rest and catch his breath. He would wander into the big kitchen and listen to the older people who sat around the large table. They talked a lot. They laughed often. Sometimes they seemed to get serious as they talked about a place they called, "The Old Country." One day he heard the story about how Valley Home got its name. The early settlers had originally called it "Tahlheim." This new country had a war with the old country and some folks who had the power to do so changed the name from "Tahl" to "Valley" and "heim" to "Home."

The rich fare of family fun was matched by lots of good food. All the kids worked in the garden alongside mother and father. The kitchen table was often loaded with the bountiful harvest. Actually most meals were what were called the "one-dish kind." A large kettle of cauliflower would feed the entire family. Eleven hungry mouths relished each bowl full of this savory vegetable. Salads varied with additions of lettuce, tomatoes, cucumbers, beans, peas, and celery. It often became the little boy's task to make the trip into the dark, damp, musty cellar to get dill pickles or sauerkraut. The farm yielded eggs, chickens, milk, butter, beef and pork. Sausage making was a yearly ritual.

As the little boy grew taller, he needed different clothes. It was exciting to see how the hand-me-downs would be passed on to the growing children. He does not remember having any new clothes until after he was in high school. Family friends who lived in a big city west of there called San Francisco would sometimes send a burlap sack of clothes. When it arrived at the local post office, it was time for a celebration. What a treat! Better than most kids feel at Christmas time. This happened any time of the year. Not often, but when the sack arrived it was memorable. As his mother carefully pulled out each garment, it became a family challenge to decide who might best fit into it. The same was true for shoes. They didn't have to fit perfectly. If there was some extra space in the toes, it could easily be stuffed with paper.

One of the boy's clearest memories was under the old hay wagon. During the cold and foggy months of winter there was less work needed in the fields, so the wagon was parked for several months beside the barn. Bundled up in mended sweaters and patched jackets, he made a small enclosure under the protection of the wagon. He carefully placed glasses, bottles, and jars on a rustic wooden shelf. He added cans and boxes. Into these treasured containers he would carefully place stuff to make an array of liquids, pastes, medicines and potions. It was as though he made magic elixirs without any idea that it wasn't possible. The leaves, seeds, mosses, twigs that made his medicines varied in color, consistency, and smells. It probably never occurred to him that he was playing at that which he might later do in reality.

True to his red-haired teacher's prediction, he did go on in school. Not only did he study in school, but he also studied in the local Lutheran Church. The teachings of Martin Luther seemed to speak to him very personally. Yes, that was it! He would answer his teacher's prediction by fulfilling his own dream. He would become a preacher. That seemed like a wonderful idea, but a different church group drew the family into a new belief and the preacher idea ended.

The new church ran a medical school. That idea seemed close enough. Maybe that would work. So he finished high school. Went on to college. Then he went through the medical school the church sponsored—Loma Linda University. He joined the Navy in one of the smaller wars the country was involved in. After that he continued his red-haired teacher's prophecy—more and more school. Ohio State University. He became a psychiatrist. His work then included teaching at Ohio State University, Loma Linda University, and the University of California in San Diego. He made some significant contributions in the field of forensic psychiatry. Along the way he raised a family of seven beautiful, happy, productive kids. They are all now married and have successful lives. He taught his children the values he had learned. Now he watches them pass these values on to his fourteen grandchildren. Perhaps the message of the old prophecy lives on. Study. Learn. Enjoy life. Be productive.

The prediction of Avis Horton 65 years ago came true. I was that little boy.

LISA TODD

Lisa Todd is an actress primarily known for her sixteen year run on the hit TV show *Hee Haw*. She has acted in numerous films and has worked with many major stars such as John Wayne in *Big Jake* and William Shatner and Ernest Borgnine in *Devil's Rain*. She has been featured on such TV shows as *The Glen Campbell Special, The Tony Orlando Show, Johnny Carson* and *Merv Griffin* to name a few. She produced and starred in three independent films and feels her experience was liberating and empowering. She enjoys the creative process and is writing a book detailing her experience in the hope it will inspire others to create their dream.

5 Tall Tale Winner
by Lisa Todd

My friend Russ and I were swapping tall tales, and he said he could outdo anything I could say. He started with—

"I've had a transplant!"

"You mean a heart attack or an actual transplant?" I asked, not believing what he had just said.

"Both," he said.

"How could that be? You're so young. When did this happen?"

"When I was 36," he said. "But it happens more often than you think."

"How did it happen?" I asked.

Russ said it was a true "B-Movie" in all its glory. "It was the worst way you would ever want to die, or the best, depending how you want to look at it—while making love. One night my wife and I were intimately involved and, when it reached a climax, it didn't stop in a normal way. Eventually, I realized I was suffering something like a minor attack.

"I tried the home remedy approach by taking some aspirin and a hot shower, but it quickly escalated into a more serious condition with sweats, nausea and a tingling arm," he said. "I told my wife to call 911, but she froze in disbelief and became disoriented. Finally, I calmed her down and convinced her this was for real and that she should make the call.

"The fire department was only a block away and I wound up in the rescue ambulance being revived with defibrillator paddles and the paramedics beating on my chest," he said. "We went to Loma

Linda Hospital where they did an angiogram and other tests to assess how bad things really were.

"After three days in the hospital, they asked me if I had ever considered a transplant. I said, 'I can't quite say I ever had.'

"That gave everyone a moment of much needed laughter. Then I looked at a picture of my kids and said, 'Okay, if that's what has to be done, let's do it.' Then the doctor said, 'Let's try a bypass first. But since you aren't strong enough we need to wait. Eat more and strengthen yourself, and we'll do it on your birthday.'"

So his 36th birthday present was going to be a six-vessel bypass. He told me his dad had been the very first patient to receive a teflon aortic valve, which was put in during a very risky and experimental operation. From those memories Russ remembered approximately how long one could be on a heart-lung machine before there was any brain damage.

Originally they were only going to do a triple bypass, but the night before the operation, they increased that to six, which meant more possible complications. But instead they decided to remove and replace his heart, and it took many more hours than they originally planned. As a result he had to be in bed for three days with his chest still open and linked up to a battery of nearby equipment.

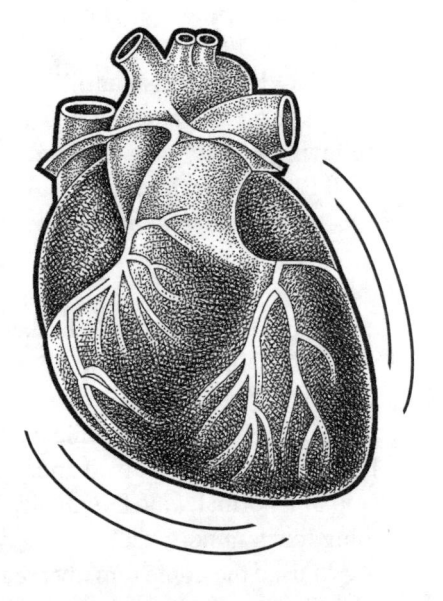

"I was in complete denial about just how sick I really was," he said. "I didn't realize how weak and disoriented I had become. They sewed me up, and after a long period of rest, I tried to return to work. But I was unable stay awake for any length of time.

UCLA informed him it would take at least two years before a heart would become available, and they rigged him up with a pager. But it wasn't too long before he got a page in the middle of the night, and they asked if he could be at the UCLA Medical Center in less than an hour. But after getting his family up and ready, another call from his doctor informed him the heart had gone bad. Later he missed another one due to a malfunction of his pager.

After a few more miscues, his doctor called and they rushed him off to UCLA.

"The staff and the beautiful environment there makes you feel completely at home. The room I was in had a fish tank, a good selection of videos, and they even brought pets around to comfort the patients. But when my wife and family visited, I had a flashback to a childhood memory. Suddenly it occurred to me where I was!"

He was occupying the same bed, same room, same floor, and the same hospital in which his father had died 23 years before. Pondering that coincidental realization, he was taken off to the operating room. Seven hours later, on Easter Sunday, April 8, 1998, he received his transplant.

"I call myself the Easter Bunny. I was resurrected. Look out world, here I come!

"The point is, you just don't give up," he said. "When I looked at my family, I realized there was too much to live for."

When it came to swapping tall tales, I had to admit I had been *completely* outdone.

VAL MIDDLEBROOK

Val Middler Middlebrook is Vice President and co-owner with her husband, Dr. R. David Middlebrook, of Ardem Associates, a company that teaches courses to Analog Engineers in industry on how to do their designs using very little math. She is also the author of *Val's Victory: Defeat Was NEVER an Option*. She can be reached at: Val@ValsVictory.com. Her book may be ordered through her web site http://www.ValsVictory.com. Dr. Middlebrook's tapes and CD ROMs can be purchased through his web site http://www.Ardem.com.

6 Angels On Our Highways
by Val Middlebrook

Strangers helping strangers has always been and always will be a part of our American life. It couldn't be more true than with the drivers of the big rigs who live on our highways. They happily stop and offer their help and expertise to motorists in trouble, using equipment of which we novices have no awareness. It has become their legacy, and I think they do it with pride.

Over the years my family has been helped several times by these "Angels On Our Highways." The first time was during World War II. I was still in high school in 1942 and '43 when our family made two trips to California. The first was to see my brother off to the Pacific with the Marines, and seventeen months later we returned to California to welcome him home. At that same time my other brother, a Marine fighter pilot, was preparing to leave for the Pacific from California's El Toro Marine Air Base. As we were driving home to Arkansas, Mother sadly said, "My two sons will never return to Little Rock." Shortly thereafter she began making plans to move permanently to California.

Because it was wartime, renting a house in Long Beach would have been virtually impossible, so we bought an 18-foot trailer to live in until we found a home. Dad had a little 1942 Studebaker to haul the trailer from Arkansas. After we loaded both car and trailer with as much as possible, we packed the rest of our belongings for shipment when we got our new address.

When we reached Arizona on the now famous Route 66, we were told that the Studebaker did not have enough horsepower to pull the loaded trailer to the top of the next mountain. Too far west to turn back, we tackled the incline with gusto, passing a rock quarry where we saw several flatbed trucks.

Sure enough, about halfway up the mountain, our poor little car could go no farther. We unloaded everything from the trailer and car and stacked it by the side of the road. Mother and I sat down on the cushions and with great relief we watched Dad slowly ascend the mountain with the empty car and trailer. I'm sure it looked like a scene from *The Grapes of Wrath.*

As we waited for Dad to return, a long empty flatbed truck pulled up beside us. Several Latino men jumped off the truck and started loading our belongings saying, "Jump on. We'll take you up the hill. When we saw you go by, we knew you would never make it." They insisted, "It's okay, we do this for people all the time!"

Mother climbed in the cab and I struggled onto the large flatbed of the truck and rode happily up the hill with these strangers—laughing all the way. When we got to the top, they helped Dad put everything back in its proper place and we were quickly on our way. I began to think there really were guardian angels.

* * *

In 1967, my husband, young son, daughter and I were in Arizona, having left Wichita Falls, Texas, to return home to Long

Beach, when we had a blowout. As my husband jacked up the car, it started to sink into the soft sandy loam of the roadside. He searched for something to support the jack and found a large rock. But each time he got the car up a little way, the jack would slip and fall back. I said, "Let's hail a trucker, they'll help us." In total disgust he said, "No, they won't even stop—much less help." After several more attempts and continued failures, I began to fear that the next time the jack slipped it might cut off his hand or arm.

Finally, seeing a big rig coming from the west, I ran toward the highway, waving my arms. The driver stopped and I explained our dilemma. Without hesitation he pulled out a large jack and said, "I'll give you a hand." As we approached the car, he said, "Let me do it!" My speechless husband stepped back, and we watched as the truck driver removed our jack and put his large jack under the axle. The car rose with ease, and he removed the wheel, replaced it in minutes and put it in its proper place in the trunk.

"You need to get a new tire as soon as possible, and I'll tell you where to get one. It may be more expensive since we're so far from a large city," he warned us, "but don't try to go on without a good spare tire—it's too risky!"

* * *

Another time returning from Little Rock, Arkansas, we awoke to heavy rain outside of Waco, Texas. Sitting on the side of the bed I suddenly had a sinking feeling, I just knew we shouldn't risk driving in that downpour.

Unable to persuade my husband to stay put until the rain subsided, we got dressed and loaded the car. The rain was torrential. We approached a bridge and picked up speed to pass a huge truck. My heart leaped and I stifled a yell—"NO!" Just as we passed the bridge we hit a large body of water in a low spot on the road and were completely blinded as the water engulfed our station wagon. My husband hit the brakes. We went into a slide and started to hydroplane.

I was in the back seat of the station wagon praying for all of us to get through safely. We were headed straight for the railing that extended the bridge. I grabbed the back of the seat and buried my face and body into it, hugging it with all my might. I prayed even harder for our survival.

Suddenly we hit the railing and I was almost thrown loose. As I held on even tighter, we hit that rail again and again. The car jumped and literally rode on top of it like a monorail for nearly 300 feet before landing upright in wet sand.

When I finally lifted my head and opened my eyes, my family was staring at me. I said, "Are you all right?" Much to my amazement the answer was, "Yes!"

"Let's get out of here before this thing explodes!" I yelled. We scrambled out in the downpour, sinking in the sand as we trudged to safety.

A trucker had already stopped and was running to us yelling "Are you all right? I've already called the Highway Patrol and they're on their way." When the officers arrived, they were shocked that no one was dead or injured. And then one added, "Whole families have been killed at this spot when they hit that water." To this day I wonder why they hadn't filled that sink hole years before.

The young trucker offered to put our car onto his truck and take us home since his truck was empty and he was on his way to Los Angeles. My husband declined his offer, and it was months before we were able to get the car back to California because of the repairs needed.

Recently my new husband and I took a trip from Los Angeles to Lake Arrowhead, Big Bear and the high desert of California. On our way home we saw smoke from a distant forest fire. It caused a huge traffic backup, blocking the freeway.

Just before we were to enter the jammed I-15, there was a truck stop loaded with dozens of 18-wheelers. Trying to figure how to get home, we were aware that truckers know the highways, and we pulled up next to one of them. He got out and came over to us and said an automobile had burst into flames on the I-15, starting a brush fire. The freeway was blocked for miles in both directions, and the truckers were all trying to figure how they were going to get around it.

When we asked how we could get to Los Angeles, he went to the cab of his truck and brought a large map book, showing us the best route to avoid the fire. He spent close to half an hour with us and made sure we wouldn't get lost in our new, round-about journey.

We've heard so much about guardian angels in books, songs, films and television. Do they really exist? I know from personal experience they are up and down the highways of this great country. These "Angels On Our Highways" have always been there to protect and assist our family, as well as many others on our busy highways, all of my life.

BERNICE SCHACHTER

Bernice Schachter, M.A. is an accomplished sculptor who has also written a motivational book *The Creative Quest*. She conducts creativity workshops in Puerto Vallarta, Mexico. For more information log on to Google Search for Bernice Schachter, or send an email to Berles@fea.net.

7 Artist at Work

by Bernice Schachter

A sign went up on the door, KEEP OUT! It was meant for me and almost ended a very close friendship. June—my muse, my mentor, my best friend—shut me out of her painting studio and her life.

Just before she placed her KEEP OUT sign on the studio door, she greeted me happily at breakfast one morning. "I'm going to quit my teaching job and unplug my phone. I need to paint undisturbed."

"Oh sure," I replied sarcastically. "What about eating? Do you propose to give that up as well as our mortgage payments?"

"Not to worry. I still have money in the bank."

I held my breath, and because I was afraid to hear her answer, I asked very softly, "And what about our collaborative writing? Will you give that up too?"

"Yes," she answered emphatically, giving me one of her familiar drop dead looks. "And don't come into the studio and nag me."

After years of a neglected painting career, June had the burning desire to be a practicing artist again. I understood her momentous decision to pursue her own muse and return to her studio. A New York gallery had promised her a showing when and if she produced a body of work.

"June is just ahead of her time," her mother had always said. Ironically, the death of her mother was the catalyst for a new beginning and for June's return to oil painting. Relieved of caretaking for her imperious mother after her demise, June found the dedication needed to be a working artist again. This meant shedding her unfocused life and times we usually spent traveling together pursuing life's frivolities and having a great time as two recently divorced and liberated women.

I certainly was curious and anxious to view what she was secretly doing behind the closed door. I was surprised by the energy that kept her going, oblivious to everything else. After a few months, she finally allowed me to enter her inner sanctum and catch a glimpse of her anguished works of art. The sight shocked me! The paintings lined up against the walls were horrendous, horrific, morbid, and bizarre; depicting June's emotions, fantasies, and creative angst. I was appalled by the dark, grotesque work that had emerged from her gut feelings. June's first creative high depicted the love-hate relationship with her mother. The mother's face was staring out of the nude womb that was a portrait of a pregnant June. There were twelve enormous paintings, six feet by four feet, painted in thick oils on large stretched canvases. Her efforts were strident, bold and sensual—typical of June herself—unforgettable.

These paintings, called "The Masks," were metaphors focusing on the mysteries of life, birth, pain, and death. In each painting June incorporated one of the masks gathered during the world travels we went on together. It was just these trips that had kept her away from the studio in the past years.

Memories, dreams, and fears were exploding in a flood of colors squeezed from the tubes of oils onto her glass palette. Applied boldly and masterfully, they were bright, unadulterated paints of alizarin crimson, yellow ochre, and vermilion joined in a cacophony of dark, black colors reminiscent of the German Expressionists or the Fauves. Her insatiable hunger for fame and immortality increased as she finished one canvas after another.

She had found her sense of place in the idle studio in our shared "Enchanted Cottage" in the San Fernando Valley. We had called it home for the past ten years. Gloating with self-glorification, she boasted to me and everyone else who knew her, "I am going to be on the cover of *Time* someday." Being her best friend, I wanted to believe it.

Her egocentric concerns with her own image were painted using a mirror to see herself as the observer in an exploration of her own life. June created her own myths in autobiographical works very much like Frida Kahlo, the famous Mexican painter. She used the language of her dreams and her unconscious mind, recreating herself as the woman behind the self-portraits that were included in each of the canvases. Possessed, she painted her vanity and ego with a full brush. In one of the paintings she depicted three women beautifully dressed in turn-of-the-century period costumes. They sit in an old-fashioned carriage, holding Japanese parasols over their heads with one hand, while the other hand partially covers the face that is a skeletal skull. The horse pulling the carriage is also a skeleton. June had an obsession for skeletons that haunted many of the works.

As the series progressed, they became too preposterous for my taste in art, but June was elated with the results. I feared June's depressing works would not be saleable and would only fill up our precious closet space. However, I did believe they were of museum quality and maybe the New York gallery would do the necessary promotion. I encouraged her by pointing this out and said the habitually wrong thing.

"Your paintings are masterpieces. A museum would love them, but can't you lighten them up a little? Make them less depressing so someone would buy them."

These provoking remarks ostracized me from her studio once again, and I found myself ignored on a daily basis. She displayed her annoyance with me by tacking a larger and bolder sign on the door, "KEEP OUT!! ARTIST AT WORK!"

Now galleries and museums are displaying artists' inner experiences, hallucinations, and fantastic imageries along with figurative paintings once ignored by the modern school of Abstract and Minimalist. I hear June's mother's voice again saying, "June is always ahead of her time."

June wasn't fun anymore. I became her jealous and displaced friend who worried about the change in her. Even more determined that her *capo di lavoro* or masterpieces would bring her recognition, she continued working on these dark, narrative paintings of the events of her life.

At that time, I had an uneasy feeling that her paintings were a sign or a warning to pay attention to the cause and not the effect of the art works. I was fearful but reluctant to say they indicated something disconcerting or distressing. June was never one to take criticism, so I didn't articulate my alarm over the premonition and uneasiness affecting me. While she indulged in this painting marathon, she made me promise not to nag her. I didn't. I just missed her.

One day I came home from teaching my sculpture class and found June hammering a large nail into our living room wall to hang her skeleton carriage ladies over our black leather couch.

"Help me," she insisted.

"I don't want to," I said. "I won't like it there. It is too morbid for our happy home."

"Life is a hell of a trade off," she replied ominously. "If this leaves the living room, so do all your marble sculptures."

This painting and others soon found places on our living room walls. My four marble sculptures remained in place to reflect upon the compromise.

June was prepared to show "The Mask" series to the gallery director, who promised to view the work on her yearly trip to Los Angeles looking for West Coast artists. The day of the appointment was a nervous time for both of us and, after we had waited all day, the woman called.

"I'm running late," she said. "I can't make it to the Valley before my plane leaves for New York, but I'll catch up with you on my next trip to L.A."

June was devastated by the cancellation and worn out by her year of intensive painting, anxiety, and expectations. She retreated to her bedroom with both physical and mental pain. After two days of a persistent stomachache, I insisted she see her doctor. He prescribed a battery of diagnostic tests. Many weeks later the verdict was IT—metastasized cancer.

June wrote in her journal that day:

I am confused with some of the facts that seem to louse up my art career. CANCER, CANCER! I find this totally unacceptable. I didn't opt for that, or did I? That's a tough question to answer, especially since I subscribe to the theory that we are in a large part responsible for our illness.

There is no possible doubt that the main part of my life was filled with stress. I remember my hair hurting. It is hard to believe it is my concern over money. Has this allowed IT to live in my body? Is that enough to trigger cancer?

I need to face the fact I'm fighting windmills as an artist. I paint primarily for the love of it. It's my life—and there may lie the answer. I have been denying myself life!

When you examine the lives of artists, so many of them suffered and died young, consumed by their passion. Being an artist may not be the healthiest way to live, ever searching, ever critical, ever striving and destroying canvas after canvas in search of a good painting. I am filled with doubts when I can't make it happen. I don't seem to have a fear of dying, and I am not frightened by the thought of it. I am just angry. It's just not my time. I had plans to live to be one-hundred-two. With medicine making wonderful and miraculous discoveries, any day there might be a cure.

June's paintings were the forewarnings recognized too late, because she was absorbed and drowning in her creative flow. I was stunned and frightened with the possibility of losing her. I only know I went to sleep that day thinking about IT and woke up distraught because my best friend could leave me living alone.

After the many tearful days that followed, I came home from teaching to find a beautifully wrapped box, tied with a yellow ribbon in my bedroom. Inside was a small note written on June's personal stationery. It said, "I, June Smith, promise to live to be 102." She might have kept her word, if only she could have reinvented herself to face life without fantasy and shed some of the many masks hiding the true June Smith. She never gave up hope and, and on her last days, made me promise to tell it like it was. There was an art to living, and we discovered there was an art to dying gracefully.

Note: *The Masks of My Muse* is a book by Bernice Schachter. It is in two parts: "The Art of Living" & "The Art of Dying."

JAMES F. HOLT

James F. Holt is a retired numerical analyst, mathematician, and scientific programmer analyst in Los Angeles. He is the mathematician who solved the mysteries of chaos mathematics, which had baffled mathematicians for over 150 years. He is a member of the Los Angeles Shakespeare Authorship Roundtable, ALAP (The Alliance of Los Angeles Playwrights), and the Book Publicists of Southern California. He has just completed a book on chaos mathematics, *Order Out of Chaos: Chaos, Fractals, and the Mandelbrot Set Explained*. His other books in progress include: *Anthony Bacon a.k.a. William Shakespeare*, *Death of a Programmer*, and *The Man Who Murdered Jack the Ripper*. He is the author of the play *To Play's the Thing*, which was produced twice at UCLA.

8 Huckleberry Holt
by James F. Holt

JULY 4TH, 2003. Los Angeles, NEWSFLASH:

A new genetic engineering breakthrough has increased the intelligence of dogs, cats, and rats such that the I.Q.s of many of these animals (especially German Shepherds, French Poodles, and Border Collies) are now equivalent or superior to the majority of the human race. Although only a few have mastered speech, some have become proficient with PCs, Microsoft Word and other word-processors, and FAX machines—and are now attempting to communicate with the outside world. Since Dear Abby has refused to answer letters from these highly intelligent animals, the author has set up an e-mail address for correspondence and to give advice to these animals. Following are several samples of this communication.

HUCKLEBERRY HOLT

FIRST GENETICALLY ALTERED DOGS, CATS, AND RATS COMMUNICATE WITH HUMANS.

Dear Huck:
I'm just a cat. However, cats have opinions, ideas, and feelings just like humans. What I'm writing about is this: Last week a new feline moved into our neighborhood. She's beautiful! I can hardly wait to make her acquaintance. However, I'm worried that my other girlfriends in the neighborhood will cut me off if I move too quickly. What is your advice?

—*Big Tom from East LA*

Dear Big Tom:

I would caution you to move slowly. Remember that old adage: "Hell hath no fury like a woman scorned." I suspect this also applies to felines. Also, remember that "a bird in the hand is worth two in the bush." However, "nothing ventured, nothing gained." Good luck!

Dear Huck:

My name is Rover (what a horrible name to give to man's best friend!). I'm writing about all the postmen who keep complaining about being bitten by dogs. I want to tell the world for the first time just why we dogs bite postmen. It's simple. They never deliver our mail. I've been living in this house for over ten years and have yet to receive a single letter. I'm in love with a French poodle that I met in Denver on our last vacation. She promised to write, but I still haven't heard from her. Don't print my last name.

—*Rover, Tarzana*

Dear Rover:

I sympathize with you 100%. When you're in love, it's horrible to wait for a letter that never comes. I was in love with a beautiful, blonde, blue-eyed girl named Irma Jean in the 5th grade, but she never noticed me. When I moved away, I never saw her again. It was terrible. I kept hoping for a letter.

However, I would advise you to be cautious about biting postmen. Although most humans are against the death penalty for themselves, they think nothing of putting dogs, cats and ducks under the ether. Just bark at the postmen. I'll pass along your message.

Dear Huck:

I'm a female cat who lives in Bel Air. I've been having an affair with a big, handsome tomcat from Westwood for over five years. He has green eyes and tiger stripes. He makes his rounds once per week. Lately, he's beginning to lose his pizzazz—if you get my meaning. What should I do?

—Had It In Bel Air

Dear Had It In Bel Air:

There's a simple way to end an affair with a cat. As you well know, every tomcat leaves his scent at each of his romantic rendezvous points. Most tomcats are not too bright. My advice is to simply erase his itinerary by putting a little catnip over his scent. Works every time. He'll rush home for a big meal and forget all about you in no time. Keep me posted.

Dear Huck:

I'm a female dog. I like your name Huckleberry. You sound like one of us. (Are you really a dog?) What I'm writing about is this: We have an old dog in our neighborhood who is going senile and is losing his eyesight—as well as most of his other body functions. The problem is that he still thinks he's Warren Beatty. He tends to jump anything that moves. How can we discourage this Bozo?

—Looking for a Young One in Glendora

Dear Looking for a Young One:
   They say you can't teach an old dog new tricks. However, it is sometimes difficult to break one of his old habits. He just doesn't get it! Since he's an old dog, my advice is to engage him in a long run every day. Invite him on a snipe hunt. Fun and games is what he needs. Before long his tongue will be hanging out of both sides of his mouth at once. He'll get the message—or die trying.

Dear Herr Huckleberry Holt:
   I am a German Shepherd dog from Heidelberg, Germany. I have been injected with the genes of the prince of mathematicians, Karl Friedrich Gauss. Recently, I have derived a new and simpler method of calculating the constant Π. Since you are a mathematician, I would be interested in your opinion. My iterator is as follows: $\Pi/6 = x_{i+1} = |x_i - |x_i/\sin(x_i)||$ for $0. < x_0 < 1$. And $x_{i+1} = 0.50*(x_{i+1} + x_i)$. Also, Aitken's delta square can be used to accelerate convergence. $\Pi/3$ can be solved by replacing $\sin(x_i)$ by $\cos(x_i)$. I am currently studying the Riemann zeta function hypothesis.
                                     —*Michael Von Schmidt from Heidelberg*

Dear Michael:
   Famous mathematicians in the past (e.g., Archimedes, Cusanus, Euler, Gauss, Ramanujan, the Borweins, etc.) have designed algorithms for finding the values of Π. However, your iterator appears to be one of the simplest. You may be interested in using the Brent and Smith multi-precision FORTRAN programs for a new world record for the number of significant figures for the constant Π. Good luck!

Dear Huckleberry:
   I'm one of those new white mice that has been genetically altered to acquire the same virus infections as humans. Listen man, I've had it with you humans! God only knows what they have injected me with. However, I've managed to escape from the laboratory in Los Alamos and am heading for Los Angeles. If you bastards think you have trouble there now, wait until I arrive. We're

all going to get into bed together. You'll all rue the day that you tangled with Los Alamos Louie.

—*Los Alamos Louie*

Dear Los Alamos Louie:
 I can understand your concerns. Listen Louie, don't do it! Don't bring the New Mexico plague into Los Angeles. We've got enough troubles. Please call me on the hot line. We can work this out. Don't become a martyr for the cause. The entire Los Angeles Police Force will be on the lookout for you and will shoot you down like a dirty rat! Surely, you have a mother or a girl friend somewhere who loves you?

JOYCE SPIZER

9 Goodbye Eye
Joyce Spizer

My Cowboys were scalping the Redskins, up fourteen points on *Monday Night Football*. What a great way to end Labor Day weekend. Husband Harold had barbecued fish in the backyard while our thirty-two-year-old son, Scott, laughed and teased me in the kitchen, taunting me with earlier memories of a Cowboys' three and eleven season.

"Go, Cowboys." I yelled.

Scott responded, "I feel an interception coming on."

The ringing phone shattered our banter.

"Hello."

"Is this the Spizer residence? Harold Spizer?"

"Yes, it is. I'm Mrs. Spizer."

An air of authority in the female's voice caused me to hesitate. I glanced out the window to see if Harold had the hands-free phone with him. He didn't.

"May I help you?"

"Thank you, yes. This is the Riverside County Sheriff's office. Do you have a son named David?"

My mouth went dry. Each heartbeat drowned out my quivering response. "Yes, we do."

We'd received a similar call from the Riverside coroner's office six years earlier during another Monday Night Football game when our eighteen-year-old son, Adam, had been found dead in his apartment.

My legs buckled under me as I remembered that horrible night and those dreadful words...son...Adam...died in his sleep... synergistic reaction to prescription medication combined with alcohol.

Adam, only eighteen, and now the oldest son David? Please God, NO.

The woman's voice droned on. "About six-thirty tonight David became the unfortunate victim of what appears to be a random physical attack at his apartment."

A wave of nausea flooded over me and I missed most of what followed.

At that moment the ambulance was preparing to transport David to the nearest trauma center. She offered me an address. I looked for something to write with. I found a broken pink crayon.

CRAYON!

"The grandkids. God. Where are my grandchildren? David is divorced and raises three children by himself. If those bastards hurt my babies...."

"No ma'am, according to my report, the neighbors have the children. They're unhurt, safe and sound. In fact, your granddaughter made the 911 call."

"What happened?"

"The witnesses told me David had been summoned to the children's pool area where two non-residents were cursing and spattering beer over the children. He tried to reason with the intoxicated men. One grabbed David from behind and held his arms, while the other viciously struck him in and about the face and body."

"How bad is David hurt?" *Do I want to know before I see him?*

"He is classified as critical. I suggest you get to Riverside County Hospital right away. David will probably need you now more than the grandchildren do."

Scott ran outside to get Harold. They entered the house in time to catch the last of my anxious comments to the investigating officer.

"What's happening?" Scott asked.

"What's wrong?" Harold hollered.

I held them off, "Ask the paramedics to tell David that his dad, brother Scott and I are on the way. Tell him to hang on." I added, "Tell him we love him."

I gripped the steering wheel as we covered the length of four freeway systems and reached the Riverside exit in record time. We passed two CHP units parked by the roadside working on their paperwork. *Thank goodness for shift changes.*

Harold ground his teeth and pounded the dashboard, "David

doesn't deserve this. He's a hardworking, honest guy, and a wonderful father."

From the back seat, Scott leaned forward and patted his dad's shoulder. "Don't forget, Dad. He's thirty-four and in great health. He's going to be fine."

The emergency-room doors automatically parted, admitting our panicky family. The smell of ammonia filled my lungs. Harold, Scott and I joined hands. I commanded my heart to be strong.

The triage nurse and investigating officer met us inside and drew us further into the depths of the hell that awaited us. She cautioned us, "He's very critical. You may tell him you love him, but please," she whispered, "try not to show emotion in his presence as it may cause him additional panic."

The nurse pulled the cubicle curtain aside.

The body lying in that bed couldn't be our son. A bloody sheet shielded his nakedness. I kissed his swollen forehead, searching the barely recognizable battered face. I raised the bloody gauze that covered the left side of his head. The eye looked grossly deformed, the inside of his skull and brain matter exposed. With each heartbeat, eye tissue and blood pumped out and rolled down his temple to the graying hairline. I shuddered.

David grabbed my hand with his left one, and his dad's with the right. He squeezed so hard I winced.

With his pain-filled whisper he pleaded, "Please don't let God take me now."

Harold leaned over the bed and whispered something. I didn't know what he said. And I've never asked. But David's body relaxed and so did his grip on my fingers.

As I stood there watching him, I thought, *David drives a truck for God's sake. That's all he knows, driving trucks. My God, how stupid of me to worry about how he's going to make a living. He may not live.*

The hospital called in an eye specialist, a neurosurgeon, and the surgical team. The miracle work began just before midnight.

We sat silently on the waiting room benches, holding on to one another. Nervously, I paced back and forth between the chapel and the surgical doors. The surgery lasted long enough for memories of David's life to pass through my mind. *All the pain of growing up. And for what? Would he make it to his thirty-fifth birthday?*

At three-thirty the next morning, the surgeon joined us with news.

"When I got into the eye itself," the doctor said flatly, "the lens was gone. David will be blind in his left eye. He may lose sight in the other. We may still lose him altogether because...."

I missed the last sentence.

***

"I love picnics, Grandma." Ryain hugged me tightly around my legs. She grows so fast, this year her hugs reach my thighs.

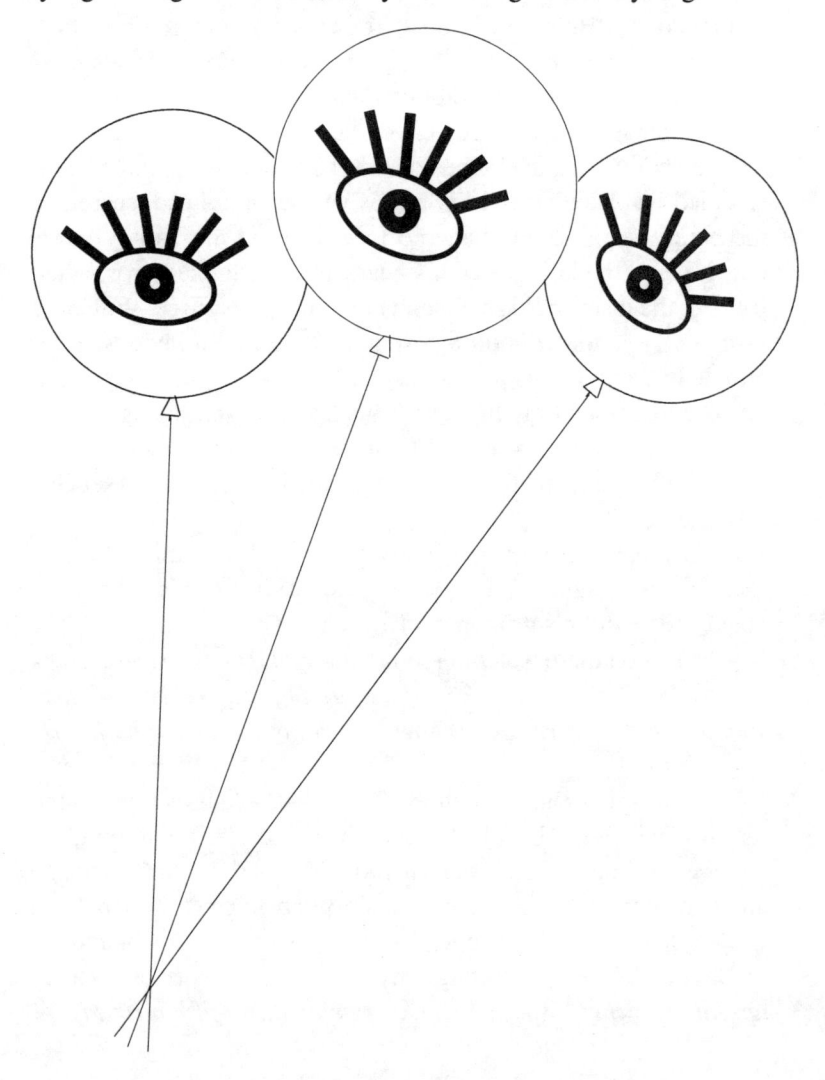

"I do too, Ry. Where's Daddy?"

"He's playing with some balloons over there in the open field. And I think, I think he's crying. I'm scared Grandma. Is he okay?"

"He's just fine." I assured her as I quickly maneuvered my way to David without alarming her.

I walk up quietly behind him, "What'sha doing?"

How's that for nonchalance?

"Painting a balloon, Maw."

"...A face?"...A message?...What?"

"An eye. My eye."

"Uh, huh." I tried to play it cool.

"I'm making one for each family member."

"Okay." I'm very cool now. "And then what?" *Were all those months of extensive counseling wasted?*

"A year has passed. The trial's behind us. The bad guys are in prison. I know the first prosthesis implant didn't take, but I have a new specialist and renewed hope. Now it's time for us to heal. We must say goodbye to my eye, Maw. Goodbye to the anger, to the fear, the pity. We have to set it free so we can go on with our lives."

When David finished painting the balloons, he gathered the rest of the family. We made a small circle, each holding our own personalized balloon, each decorated with one giant eye.

After a brief, silent prayer, and a count of one, two, three, we said, "Goodbye" and set our balloons free.

They sailed away toward heaven and Adam.

ELLEN REID

10 The Meaning of Life Is Dinner
by Ellen Reid

In some families—maybe you came from one similar to mine—life seems to revolve around dinner. Sure, it looked like the focus was food, but it was more about dinner. When I was a little girl growing up I remember so much of our family life was spent exploring this subject.

Whoever was still home in the morning would start out the day at breakfast, and what did we talk about? Dinner. We enthusiastically speculated about what we were going to have for dinner; who would be there, what we should wear, was it a special occasion, and, if so, where might we be going, and so on. There were endless possibilities for discussion about—dinner.

As I grew into a young adult I started turning up my nose at this insipid subject matter. How important could dinner be when there were wars, and hatred, and injustices in the world. Oh, sure, we skirted those issues, but we never really got into the meat and bones of politics or literature or music. I'm being brought up in a "cultural wasteland!" I often observed as I lay awake nights pondering the real meaning of life.

Then, when I reached full adulthood and started a family of my own, I made a startling discovery: When my family gathered around the table, what we were actually saying really had little to do with food. We weren't really talking about dinner. We were saying how much we loved and cared for each other.

I realized that food was an excuse to create a time for people to come together, to celebrate, to commiserate, to elucidate, to pontificate! It was a time when those of us who lived alone—the grown kids, the widowed aunt, the bachelor cousin—got to be with others, and when those of us who still lived under the same roof got a chance to be together, to talk to each other and share warmth and caring and beauty. That's one of the big reasons why people set a lovely table, light candles, have floral centerpieces and why the good smells coming from the kitchen set such vivid memories in place. It's not about the food. It's about a much deeper nourishment.

"Dinner" is a priceless opportunity to be in the presence of the people we care about so we can share with them that we are living the life we love.

If you are lucky enough to come from a culture where food seems to be the focus, see if you can get past the obvious. Go deeper. Listen, taste, smell, talk, share…and love. It's a good thing. It's a great thing.

Ellen Reid
Founder of Smarketing-Infinite Possibilities
www.smarketing.com

DR. MICHAEL and (father) NED FENLON

11 The Bridge Builder
by Michael Fenlon, M.D.

Being five years old was not a good time in the life of my father, Ned Fenlon. It was during this time that his father, James, who was only 32, contracted a case of pneumonia which developed into tuberculosis. James had fought a fire at his family's store in Hessel, Michigan, in the middle of a harsh winter night, and fallen gravely ill. As a result, when Ned was about five years old, he and his parents had to leave his two younger sisters and a brother and move from Hessel to Phoenix in the Arizona Territory. This area had been suggested as having a healthier climate than the northern Michigan peninsula where Ned had been born. But after less than a year in Phoenix, Ned's father's condition took a turn for the worse and he died.

To complicate matters further, six-year-old Ned lost his voice at this same time. Polyps were discovered on his vocal chords as the result of a rare infection, and, although it might have easily been misdiagnosed as cancer, fortunately it was not. It affected his speech so that he could only whisper.

Returning to their family roots in Hessel, his mother, Anna, and his uncle took over the family grocery business known as The Fenlon Brothers Store. It had been rebuilt during their stay in Arizona. It was a very popular center in the little town and its reopening was warmly welcomed. In addition to Ned losing his voice, he also was severely nearsighted. A teacher later recommended glasses, and a whole new world of sight opened up to Ned. But in spite of these handicaps, Ned was given many adult responsibilities due to the loss of his father.

His mother continued the long-standing family tradition of

welcoming members of the Ottawa and Chippewa Indian tribes as customers, always extending them full credit when the winters were harsh and money was scarce. She was so revered they gave her the Indian name of Chicadoque meaning "blue skies" because of her deep blue eyes. Their mutual respect and friendship grew, even to inviting the family to participate in special tribal ceremonies and events.

One day, after he turned 12, the always-whispering Ned unexpectedly "shouted" a greeting to his friend Bill Blackbird in the native Indian tongue as he passed by the Fenlon home. Ned learned the language of the Chippewa and Ottawa tribes—the names of the store items, the produce, and how to count—in order to work in the family store, a skill he still possessed at the age of 99. Blackbird was startled into a state of euphoria when he realized his young friend had suddenly regained his voice. He suggested to the tribal elders that they declare it to be a special day of thanksgiving. Thus Ned was honored and celebrated for the recovery of his voice with tribal dancing and chanting in full costume, and their rituals of joy and gratitude were performed throughout that never-to-be-forgotten day in Ned's young life. His love for these special friends deepened into an enduring association throughout his long and distinguished career.

His ambition had been to go to Notre Dame since the day one of his older cousins, whom he admired and who was a student there, began talking about it. But he needed to earn his way there and took a job working on the Carlisle estate. The estate was in Mishawaka, Indiana, near South Bend. Carlisle was the head of the Studebaker Corporation, a great admirer of Notre Dame, and the Studebaker roadster he gave Ned to use was one of the very few cars allowed on the Notre Dame campus at that time.

My father graduated from Notre Dame in 1927, the year of the famous football Four Horsemen of Notre Dame—Harry Stuhldreher, Jim Crowley, Elmer Layden and Don Miller. In his last year there Ned studied in Notre Dame's law school, then pursued further training in the law at the University of St. Louis.

Ned also worked in various other jobs to support himself and earn tuition, including selling Fuller Brushes door-to-door, working in Mertaugh's Chris-Craft boat sales in Hessel, working on boats and helping to pilot them up to Hessel from the Chris-Craft boat works in Algonac, Michigan, on the southern shores of Lake Huron and Lake St. Clair. About this time he was offered the possibility of running the speedboat owned by the Grand Hotel on Mackinac Island. He jumped at the opportunity since it involved piloting a speedboat with a 250-horsepower V-8 engine, a real thrill

for him to command such power.

One of his jobs for the Grand Hotel was piloting the hotel's speedboat across the lake to Mackinaw City to get the newest editions of the *Chicago Tribune* and race them back to Mackinaw Island for the guests at the hotel. The hotel's owners prided themselves on always providing guests with the most up-to-date news.

On these daily trips Ned had a habit of taking friends and their children with him as he sped across the water. This became the most exciting and the most popular part of his job, and the children of an old family friend Prentiss M. Brown, a U.S. Congressman and later U.S. Senator, were frequent guests on these speedboat rides. So later, when the job as an apprentice in Brown's new law office in St. Ignace became available, any competition for the position disappeared after Brown's children campaigned for their friend Ned. He became an apprentice with Brown's firm and was able to take the bar exam and pass it. All this happened between 1927 to 1933.

Ned had an opportunity to run for the state legislature. Their state representative had committed suicide and, with less than two weeks remaining before the election, Ned mounted a vigorous campaign and won.

Beginning at the age of 30, he served for six years in the Michigan Legislature from 1933 to 1939. He married my mother Jane that last year. Among the bills he sponsored were those to authorize the building of three very vital bridges: the Blue Water Bridge at Port Huron, Michigan to Sarnia, Ontario, Canada; the International Bridge at Sault Sainte Marie, Michigan, to Sault Sainte Marie, (the "Soo"), Ontario, Canada; and the Mackinac Bridge (at the Straits of Mackinac), St. Ignace, Michigan to Mackinaw City, Michigan. These bridges would shorten automobile travel between the upper and lower peninsulas of Michigan and Canada to only a few minutes, whereas it took the ferry, that had to be loaded with about 50 autos, over 45 minutes to make each crossing. The waiting traffic was jammed up for hours every morning and evening.

Ned continued to work with engineers from the San Francisco Golden Gate Bridge project, circa 1937, even after leaving the legislature. Ned was appointed prosecuting attorney for Mackinac County, where he worked from 1939 to 1943. Jane and Ned moved to St. Ignace where I was born in 1940. Then they moved to open a new law office in Detroit, renamed Brown, Fenlon and Babcock. From there he was appointed a circuit judge in 1951 serving the three county area—Mackinac in the Upper Peninsula, and Cheboygan and Emmet in the Lower Peninsula of Michigan until 1974. He moved his family from Detroit to Petoskey, all this time continuing his persistent pursuit of bridge building.

Finally, the Mackinac bridge projects began. The cost was a hundred million dollars from the early planning in 1935 in the legislature to final fruition in 1954. It took Ned Fenlon's tenacious leadership to make it happen. The commercial benefits up and down the peninsulas, even affecting the economies of Wisconsin, Canada, and other surrounding states, have been incalculable.

When Ned retired in 1974 at the age of 72, he could look back on a lifetime of achievement and the building of bridges, both structural and personal. From a humble early childhood when he lost his father, becoming mute and nearly blind, he created a century of life-long friendships including the Chippewa and Ottawa Indians. His persistent efforts with legislators over the years, both as lawmaker and judge, finally saw his bridge-building legislative efforts bear fruit.

Ned Fenlon has given the state of Michigan a very large and tangible legacy.

BEVERLY BACON

Beverly (Jarvis) Bacon is originally from Kettering, OH and is currently working as a freelance photographer in Los Angeles, CA. She may be contacted at baconphoto@earthlink.net.

12 Looking Forward to 30
by Beverly Bacon

It was in the midst of the Great Depression, in the early 1930s. With the struggles of virtually no work and little food, times were very tough and very morose. People did the best they could to provide for their families despite the tremendous economic setbacks.

Trying to maintain a job and put food on the table was a full-time job in itself, but for one special young lady there was another issue she was deeply concerned about—being pregnant with her first-born child in a time of so much uncertainty.

Normally, this should be the most joyful time of one's life, expecting your first child, but there was something even more traumatic than the Depression that put a damper on this joyous occasion. The young woman's husband unexpectedly walked out on her and their unborn child.

Heartbroken, the young woman gave birth to a healthy baby girl. They both moved in with a friend who assisted in caring for the baby. Over the course of the next two years, the mother, still grief stricken over the loss of her husband, fell ill and died at the tender age of 29. The child was two years old, without a mother or a father.

Fortunately for the little girl, her aunt took her into her home to raise her. Back then it was unusual for a single woman to get custody of a child, but she managed to do it.

This incredible woman not only took the child into her home, but she gave up the man she loved and was to marry because he wanted to put the child into a foster home. When she refused to give up the girl, her fiancé left. Years later she did marry a gentleman more to be the father to her girl than because she loved him as a mate.

Despite the hardships that occurred, the two had a good life until the young girl turned sixteen. She suddenly became ill and was unsure of what was happening. She began to have problems moving her arms and legs, which understandably caused great concern and fear. Shortly afterwards, she found out she had poliomyelitis.

It took quite awhile to recuperate from this paralyzing disease, both mentally and physically. She was fortunate that she did regain the use of her legs and one arm, but sadly she was unable to use her left arm. How traumatic this must have been for a teenager to endure.

The amazing thing was she never harped on her illness and handicap. As a matter of fact, she never saw it as such. Very few people even knew anything was wrong.

Years later she met and married a wonderful, caring man who overlooked her disability. I think, too, for the first time in her life she felt like she was deeply loved and wanted, in spite of the loving sacrifices of her aunt.

She continued on to raise four children and take care of the home, along with numerous animals. Four kids are a lot for anyone to care for, let alone someone who had the use of only one arm. Again, she never complained and gave out more love than anyone I ever knew.

To grow up knowing that your own father didn't want to stay around long enough to even see you born is an extremely difficult thing to understand. Losing a mother at the age of two and never knowing her is incomprehensible. Her grandmother ironically passed away at the age of 29, the same age as her mother. I think she was one of the few women who actually looked forward to turning 30!

Today you constantly hear about people, especially women, who have issues regarding not being close with their fathers. These people spend their entire lives blaming their current situations on the fact that their father was not there for them. They feel they cannot develop close relationships with men because of that.

Not only did this woman never use that excuse, she turned out to be one of the most compassionate, loving and caring women around. To overcome such a harsh beginning in life and to end up with such a loving, giving family, this woman had to have done something right.

I know she felt at one point she had always wanted to be an expert at something, but felt she never attained that. I have to tell her that she did, in fact, reach that goal. She is an expert wife, mother and human being. She passed on all of her wonderful qualities to her four children. I should know—I am her youngest.

WINK MARTINDALE

13 The Night Music Changed
by Wink Martindale

It was Thursday night, July 8, 1954. By happenstance I was at the station that night showing some friends the studio at WHBQ where I worked. They were excited about meeting Dewey Phillips. Little did they know they were to get more than they bargained for.

Dewey Phillips, one of the top disk jockeys in Memphis and host of the *Red Hot and Blue* show from 9 p.m. to midnight, had begun playing a new record. From the first playing of the record, the phone lines lit up. He would play one side, then flip it and play the other side, over and over. The listeners couldn't get enough of this new sound.

Earlier that evening, Sun Records' founder Sam Phillips, no relation to Dewey, brought in an advanced "pressing" of a record by his new truck-driving singer, Elvis Presley.

Sam had first met Elvis when the boy had walked into his Memphis Recording Service to make a recording of "My Happiness" as a birthday present for his mother. Sam had often said, "If I can ever find a white man who sounded like a Negro, I'll make a million dollars!" In Elvis he felt he'd found that person. After over a year of rehearsing and searching for just the right songs, Sam Phillips felt "That's All Right, Mama" and "Blue Moon of Kentucky" were the ticket.

No one there that night, least of all Dewey Phillips, had any way of knowing we were witnessing the birth of a musical icon, a legend in every sense of the word—and the birth of rock 'n' roll.

Naturally as the excitement mounted, Dewey wanted Elvis to come to the station. But where was he? A call was placed to his mother who said her son had gone to the movies. Elvis had known

Phillips would be playing his record that night, but he was too nervous to listen. He was found sitting alone in a dark theater and had to be coaxed into coming to WHBQ.

Elvis seemed to be just as shocked as everybody else at the commotion he was causing. Being unaware he was on a live microphone, he began answering questions that Phillips thought were some of the things everybody wanted to hear. Nervously, Elvis was giving his very first interview as a professional entertainer. He later confided that since he had no idea the interview was on the air, he made it through. Otherwise he would never have been able to talk!

The next day, a company named Music Sales, Sun Records' distributor in Memphis, was deluged with calls for this new Elvis Presley recording. Its veteran manager, Bill Fitzgerald, told me he had never experienced such a reaction to a record. Joe Coughi, who owned one of the largest one-stop retail record outlets in the city, Home of the Blues, said he could easily have sold and shipped over 10,000 records the next day, if he'd had them to sell. The problem was, nobody (least of all Sam Phillips) anticipated the kind of reaction this new singer had generated *overnight*. It was far beyond his wildest expectations.

This first record would prove to be only a regional hit for Elvis. Although word was spreading about him far and wide, there were still many disbelievers. His first nationwide hit would come only after RCA record executive Steve Sholes negotiated the purchase of Elvis' contract from Sam Phillips and Sun Records. The price—$35,000. It was the biggest steal since the Louisiana Purchase.

His first RCA release, "Heartbreak Hotel," forever put to rest any doubt about his ability to meet and surpass the expectations of even his harshest critics. The rest, as they say, is history.

Between his early tours, and all during his professional career, Elvis always used his beloved Memphis as home base. He loved his roots, and he revered his mother.

During one of Elvis' visits home, I was able to persuade Dewey Phillips to approach him, by now a HUGE star. Though I was an acquaintance of Elvis, I knew my best bet was to work through Dewey. I appealed to my friendship with Dewey (and his ego) to join Elvis on an upcoming Milk Fund charity appearance he was about to make and conduct a joint interview with both Elvis and Dewey. He loved the idea, and convinced Elvis to do it.

At the time I was the host of a teen television show called *Top Ten Dance Party*. It was similar to *American Bandstand*, and I suppose I was known as the Dick Clark of Memphis. I discovered that when Elvis was home with his parents, they all watched the show.

Word quickly spread about the impending guest shot on *Dance Party*. The station had to hire security guards to handle the excess crowd that day. Even many of the station employees suddenly found a reason to work—*on a Saturday!*

Since there was no video recording equipment yet at WHBQ-TV in 1956, I hired a local photographer to set up a kinescope of what was, without question, the first recorded interview with Elvis on television. That filmed interview later proved invaluable to me as Elvis' fame continued to grow worldwide.

A teenaged truck driver recorded a song as a birthday present for his mother and became the greatest entertainer of the twentieth century—*only in America!*

LAEL LITTKE

Leal Littke lives with four arrogant cats who tolerate her as long as she keeps the can opener humming. She (and the cats) can be reached at: LaelJL@aol.com.

14 Diamonds In My Backyard
by Lael Littke

When I was a child I was convinced that all authors were already dead. Somehow I couldn't connect books with real, live, breathing people. When I finally learned that authors did indeed walk around like normal folks, I elevated them to the realms of the gods. And I wanted to be one.

But I was an Idaho farm girl. I'd never been more than fifty miles away from the high mountains whose canyons cradled our tiny village of Mink Creek. We were all pretty much alike there. Most of the people were of Danish descent, their ancestors having been scooped out of Denmark by Mormon missionaries in the later 1800s. Though strong and progressive and dedicated to education, they possessed a looming distrust of "the outside world."

So I grew up knowing mountains and creeks and where the wild gooseberries grew. I knew horses and cows and chickens and how magpies built their nests. But what did I know of the world? What did I know of life? How could I be a writer, an author of books, without knowing of these things? What did I have to say?

A teacher named Emil Larsen came to our small country school. His specialty was English grammar. He taught us farm kids about split infinitives and dangling participles. He taught us about future perfect tense and imperative mode and active and passive voice. He made us diagram sentences until the entire expanse of blackboard was filled with lines connected to other lines, showing the bones of the language. We might never lose our Idaho twangs, he declared, but by golly our grammar would be flawless.

He made us write, too. I wrote about the dog fight between the Hansens' and the Larsens' dogs where the only casualty was little

Eddie who got so excited he choked on his chewing gum then barfed all over everybody when they pounded him on the back. I scribbled a tale about the time the neighborhood kids were playing Run Sheep Run on a soft summer night and I fell into the spring that supplied water for my family and several others. I spoke of how I stood there shivering and wondering if they would still drink the water after they fished out my poor, drowned body. Mr. Larsen said I might be a writer. "You handle humor well, Lael," he said, "which is unusual for a seventh grader." His praise inspired me to write stories that tattled all the secrets of my dozens of cousins whose escapades were legion and sometimes lurid.

I dreamed of being a writer. One of my chores was to ride my horse each evening down along the creek, then up over the shoulder of a mountain to a high pasture and bring home our cows which spent the summer days grazing there. I dreamed my dreams as I gazed out over the valley and those endless encircling blue hills. Someday I would be like the bear who went over the mountain to see what he could see. Someday I would go out and find things I could write about. As my old gray horse jogged along following the cows, I dreamed of how it would be. I would live in a penthouse in New York City. I knew about New York from movies. My mother and Aunt Mahalia loved movies. They piled us kids three deep into our old brown Ford and took us to the Grand Theatre in Preston each time the movie changed.

Along with my penthouse I would have a magnificent car, probably a Buick, which was about as luxurious as my imagination could supply. I would wear tight leopardskin pants, and I would date Cary Grant for elegant soirees at the Copacabana (I knew about that from the movies). I would be an author.

I left my mountains to go to college in Logan, Utah, with a population of 16,000, which seemed like a vast city to me. There, Professor Moyle Q. Rice liked my sophomore compositions and encouraged me to pursue my dream. After graduation, I went to Denver (getting closer to New York City!) to be a career girl and find out how to be an author.

In Denver I met a handsome young man named George Littke whose ambitions as well as his intelligence and pleasant personality attracted me. When he asked me to marry him, I said no. I said

I had this goal of becoming a writer and I wasn't sure how that would mix with being a good Mormon wife. He said he was glad I had ambitions and that he would help me. We got married.

Miracle of miracles, just five months after the wedding George was offered a fellowship to finish studying for his Ph.D. in political science at no less than New York University in NEW YORK CITY! My dreams were coming true!

We went to live in New York City. Not in a penthouse, to be sure, but our apartment in Queens was adequate. We didn't have the Buick I'd dreamed of, but our sagging old green Dodge got us where we needed to go. I didn't date Cary Grant, but who wanted to? I had George. And there were no elegant soirees at the Copa. We did occasionally go out for a movie and a 10 cent hamburger at White Castle.

Best of all, I found a night writing class at City College of New York that I could go to after work.

But what could I write about? I still knew nothing that could snag the attention of an editor. So I wrote of Grandma Feeney who for her entire married life had saved the embroidered and crocheted pillowcases and sheets from her wedding trousseau for "company best," but never considered anyone important enough to use them. I wrote about a pink-cheeked cowboy named Snookie who fell in love with the new schoolteacher but got into trouble when he tried to attract her by riding a cranky old rodeo horse named Snort.

I was embarrassed when Ms. Frazier, the teacher, read my offerings aloud in class. The other students responded well, laughing in the appropriate places. But they were writing sophisticated stuff, about interesting people in the big city who killed each other and engaged in kinky sexual activities that were news to me.

One night Ms. Frazier asked me to stop by her desk after class.

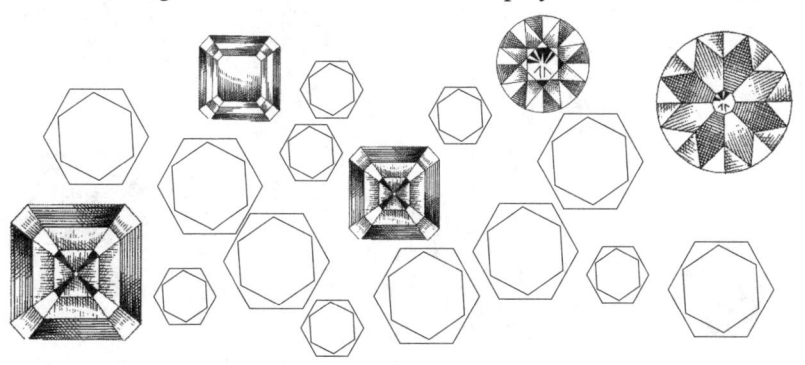

When I stood there, trembling with apprehension, she said, "You could be a successful writer, Lael, if you would write about real life."

My face flushing with embarrassment, I confessed that what I wrote about *was* real life to me. It was the only life I knew.

She gazed at me for a full minute before saying, "You're very lucky, Lael."

Lucky. Lucky? Lucky!

I read a book once titled *A Whack on the Side of the Head* by Roger van Oech, that said sometimes it takes a whack, usually figurative, to bring things into focus for those too obtuse to see what is staring them right in the face. I realized that I was a living example of the old story about the man who travels all over the world looking for great treasure but returns home empty-handed and discouraged, only to find diamonds in his own backyard.

Suddenly I saw my little village back in the mountains of Idaho as a treasure, a flowing fountain of ideas and characters and truths.

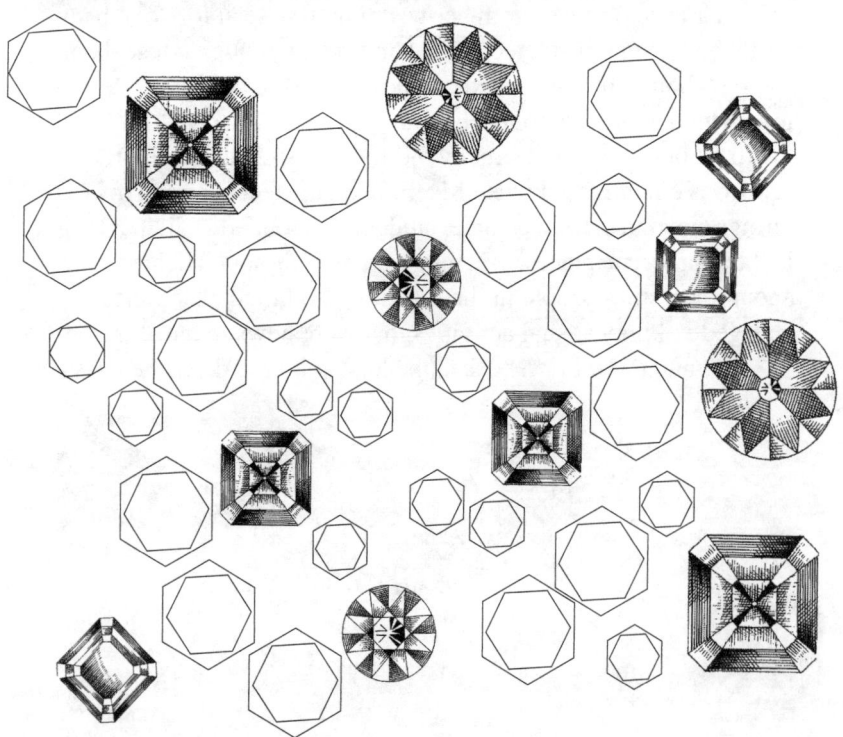

I sold the story about Grandma Feeney to a denominational magazine. Soon I began writing—and selling—teenage books set in my little hometown, changing its name for each novel so that I could use it over and over again and also because I didn't want the residents to say, "Hey, that didn't happen here in Mink Creek." I used the mountains and streams as my settings, and I used the people, combining characteristics so that nobody would recognize themselves, as my casts. I drew from the wisdom of those good people, and I included their rollicking humor. I plunked the old haunted house into one book, along with the small white tombstone that marked the grave of two little brothers who drowned in Bear River. I used horses I had known, and cats who remained in my memory. I constructed country-girl protagonists who came of age, as I did, as they journeyed from mistaken suppositions to mature realizations. I resurrected some of the tales I had told in the seventh grade, and I used them again, silently thanking Mr. Emil Larsen for teaching me how to use the language and offering me encouragement.

I have reached my dream of becoming an author and have dozens of books to my credit now. Each year I return to that small village in the Idaho mountains, and I bring away new ideas for plots and themes. I have indeed found diamonds in my own backyard.

But I never did find myself a good pair of leopardskin pants.

DR. EUGENE MANUSOV

DR. BILL FRANK

15 A Red Marble

Eugene Manusov, D.D.S.

In over fifty years of dental practice I have yet to meet a more selfless, generous colleague than Dr. Bill Frank. The following story by an anonymous author is one of my favorites. When I first heard it, I immediately thought of Bill, shared it with mutual friends, and they all agreed.

During the waning years of the depression in a small southeastern Idaho community, I used to stop by Mr. Miller's roadside stand for farm-fresh produce as the season made it available. Food and money were still extremely scarce and bartering was used extensively.

One particular day Mr. Miller was bagging some early potatoes for me. I noticed a small boy, delicate of bone and feature, ragged but clean, hungrily appraising a basket of freshly picked green peas. I paid for my potatoes but was also drawn to the display of fresh green peas. I am a pushover for creamed peas and new potatoes.

Pondering the peas, I couldn't help overhearing the conversation between Mr. Miller and the ragged boy next to me.

"Hello, Barry. How are you today?"

"H'lo, Mr. Miller. Fine, thank ya. Jus' admirin' them peas... sure look good."

"They are good, Barry. How's your Ma?"

"Fine. Gittin' stronger alla' time."

"Good. Anything I can help you with?"

"No, Sir. Jus' admirin' them peas."

"Would you like to take some home?"
"No, Sir. Got nuthin' to pay for 'em with."

"Well, what have you to trade me for some of those peas?"

"All I got's my prize marble here."

"Is that right? Let me see it."

"Here 'tis. She's a dandy."

"I can see that. Hmmmm, only thing is this one is blue and I sort of go for red. Do you have a red one like this at home?"

"Not 'zackley...but almost."

"Tell you what. Take this sack of peas home with you and next trip this way let me look at that red marble."

"Sure will. Thanks, Mr. Miller."

Mrs. Miller, who had been standing nearby, came over to help me. With a smile she said, "There are two other boys like him in our community, all three from very poor circumstances. Jim just loves to bargain with them for peas, apples, tomatoes or whatever. When they come back with their red marbles, and they always do, he decides he doesn't like red after all and he sends them home with a bag of produce for a green marble or an orange one, perhaps."
I left the stand, smiling to myself, impressed with this man.
A short time later I moved to Colorado, but I never forgot the story of this man, the boys and their bartering. Several years went by, each more rapidly than the previous one. Just recently I had the occasion to visit some old friends in that Idaho community and, while I was there, learned that Mr. Miller had died. They were having his viewing that evening and, knowing my friends wanted to go, I agreed to accompany them.
Upon our arrival at the mortuary, we fell into line to meet the relatives of the deceased and to offer whatever words of comfort we could. Ahead of us in line were three young men, one in an Army uniform, the other two wearing dark suits and white shirts—very professional looking. They approached Mrs. Miller, standing smiling and composed by her husband's casket. Each of the young men hugged her, kissed her on the cheek, spoke briefly with her and moved on to the casket. Her misty

light blue eyes followed them as, one by one, each young man stopped briefly and placed his own warm hand over the cold pale hand in the casket.

As they left the mortuary, they awkwardly wiped their eyes. When our turn came to meet Mrs. Miller, I told her who I was and mentioned the story she had told me about the marbles. Eyes glistening, she took my hand and led me to the casket. "Those three young men who just left were the boys I told you about. They just told me how they appreciated the things Jim traded them. Now, at last when Jim could not change his mind about color or size, they came to pay their debt.

"We've never had a great deal of the wealth of this world," she confided, "but right now Jim would consider himself the richest man in Idaho." With loving gentleness she lifted the lifeless fingers of her deceased husband. Resting in his hand were three, exquisitely shined red marbles.

"Life is not measured by the breaths
we take, but by the moments that take our breath."

This, and other philosophies, motivate my friend Bill Frank. In 1985 he added to his many accomplishments by becoming a part of a team of Rotarians, who then raised the initial goal of 120 million dollars to eradicate the polio virus throughout the world. Part of Bill's reason for accepting the challenge was his wife Ruth's battle with the crippling disease. She contracted polio shortly after they were married and endured a two-year hospital confinement, followed by a lengthy rehabilitation.

By the year 2000, 90 percent of children throughout the world had been immunized with the Sabin oral polio vaccine. As a result, the incidence of the disease was reduced by 99 percent. Rotary International and the United Nations set a final goal of total eradication by the year 2005.

"Many great things can be accomplished if nobody cares who gets the credit."

DR. ROBERT WEST

16 West's Point
by Robert West, D.D.S.

It was the summer of 1950. There were 48 stars in our nation's flag and a former haberdasher named Harry Truman was President of these United States. I had not, as yet, heard of such things as smog or hippies, and our favorite TV show was "Time for Beany."

Somehow, I had made it through my sophomore year at the USC Dental School. After two years in Los Angeles' famous old Flatiron Building, we, the members of the class that would, hopefully, be graduating in 1952, found ourselves in that architectural masterpiece, the Clinic Building at 16th and Los Angeles Streets. The guys in Section One (from A to M) were assigned to the Operative Clinic. Section Two (my group, from N to Z) was assigned to the second floor Prosthetics (false teeth) Clinic.

I have to assume that Dr. Vaughn (known affectionately as "The Sheriff") took an immediate dislike to me, since he assigned me to a patient named Morris Laibman, who was a retired tailor by trade. Mr. Laibman was my introduction to clinical dentistry. I was told by "The Sheriff" that I was to construct full upper and lower dentures for Mr. Laibman.

My Student Number was 291, which appeared on the name badge we were all required to wear. Mr. Laibman always referred to me as "Vest, Two-Ninety-Vun." On my very first appointment with Morris, he brought in a cigar box full of old dentures. "Vest, Two-Ninety-Vun," he said. "Dese are mine old plates. None a dem fit!"

If I had not been so naive, I would have immediately dropped out of dental school and gone into selling water heaters in my dad's plumbing shop in Southwest L.A. But as I said, this was my introduction to clinical dentistry. Fortunately, there was a recent graduate from the class of '50 who was a clinical instructor and he counseled with me. If it hadn't been for Dr. Carlson, I could be selling water heaters *today*.

I went through all the motions of trying to get primary and final impressions on Morris. From time to time, Morris would give me some instruction in what I was trying to do. He would inform me, "Vest, Two-Ninety-Vun, I got a lotta experience in choppers. Dis is the vay you should do it!"

The summer wore on, and it was getting close to the end of Section Two's assignment in the Prosthetics Clinic. I must have made ten, maybe twelve attempts, trying to get Mr. Laibman's approval. He kept saying, "Dey just don't feel right." And then he would pull one of his old dentures out of the cigar box and show me what he wanted. The *coup de grace* came one day in mid-August when Morris, the Tailor, showed up for his morning appointment with a tablespoon in hand.

"Vest, Two-Ninety-Vun, you see dis spoon?" I nodded, trying to figure out where this was going. Mr. Laibman put the tablespoon, convex side up, in the roof of his mouth and held it there for a few seconds. He removed the spoon and said, "Dat spoon fits my gooms poifict. Make da plate like dat and it will be poifict."

I said, "Mr. Laibman, excuse me. I have to talk to the instructor." I immediately went over and got in the long line of students who were following our instructor, Dr. Carlson, around the second floor. When he finally got to me, I just said, "You've got to see this to believe it." Knowing Morris, the Tailor, as well as I, he smiled and followed me to Morris's side.

"Mr. Laibman," I inquired, in a voice trying to stifle my emotions, "would you show the doctor what you just demonstrated for me with that tablespoon?"

Morris complied. Dr. Carlson didn't flinch. He took the tablespoon from Mr. Laibman and asked, quite matter-of-factly, "Mr. Laibman, do you want us to set the denture teeth up on this spoon?"

From that day forward, my savior, Dr. Ed Carlson, checked me out and I got a "Finish Check" for my first set of dentures, which Mr. Laibman quickly added to the collection in his cigar box.

Later that fall, when the Junior Class from Section Two was allowed to enter the Operative Clinic on the first floor, I heard that "The Sheriff" had assigned Morris Laibman to a senior from Section One, who was considered a "prosthetics whiz."

I don't mean to gloat, but I heard later from a classmate in Section One that the "Whiz's" dentures also ended up in Morris, the Tailor's, cigar box.

Dr. Robert West graduated from the USC School of Dentistry in 1952. Fifteen years earlier, in 1937, one of the greatest heroes of World War II, Dr. Benjamin L. Salomon, also graduated from USCSD. Captain Salomon gave his life by singlehandedly fighting off at attack by thousands of the enemy to save hundreds of wounded and his fellow regimental soldiers on the island of Saipan on the 7th of July, 1944.

Dr. West spent five years in an attempt to win Captain Salomon a highly deserved posthumous Medal of Honor. Finally, in the spring of 2002, President George W. Bush signed the order to award the medal to Captain Salomon, and Dr. West accepted the honor on his behalf. On the first day of May, 2002, in the White House Rose Garden, Captain Salomon was awarded the nation's highest honor for valor, ending fifty-eight years of frustrated attempts to recognize his great sacrifice.

CAPT. BENJAMIN L. SALOMON, D.D.S.

The Ballad of Captain Ben

Doctor Ben of USC
Earned his D.D.S. degree.
He joined the Army infantry
Just to serve, like you and me.

Earned his stripes by training men.
They all followed Sergeant Ben.
He would treat them like a friend,
Or treat their teeth to help them mend.

In '41, that fateful day,
Burning ships across the bay.
World War II was underway.
Ben's at Fort Ord in Monterey.

He is now Lieutenant Ben.
Still he treats and trains his men.
In 1944 he's sent
To Saipan with his regiment.

One day, he was treating wounds,
The enemy, in a large platoon,
Attacked his tent and very soon
He saw that everyone was doomed.

Captain Ben faced the attack.
Yelled "Save the men. I'll be right back."
All by *himself* he turned them back
And gave his life in that attack.

Captain Ben, like Roger Young,
Died for men he marched among.
Some go unsung, no honors won.
We honor <u>*now*</u> Ben Salomon.

by Ernie Weckbaugh

DR. ROGER LEIR

Dr. Leir is a world-renowned investigator in ufology, and has authored numerous books including *The Aliens and the Scalpel* and *Casebook Alien Implants* regarding alien implants in humans. He has appeared on numerous radio and television programs and presented to audiences worldwide. Visit his website: Alienscalpel.com or his email: RKLeir1st@aol.com.

17 Alone In a Universe
(a true story)
by Roger Leir, D.P.M.

Have you ever asked the question, "Are we the only intelligent life in our universe?" Well, I have and the answer was driven into my mind as if someone had hammered a nail into my brain. It happened one night as I stood with my wife and young daughter to look at the heavens. Suddenly we saw the stars move. The shock and telepathic message that followed changed my life forever.

Later we walked inconspicuously between the tables of the banquet hall. My wife and nine year old daughter were at my side. I had decided to give up our seats in the middle of the EBE Video Award Ceremony. As we approached the doorway my wife whispered loudly, "Why in hell are we leaving? What in God's name are you doing now?"

I responded with dead silence. I could feel her anger beginning to enshroud me like an invisible envelope. We made our way through a small crowd of people. Arriving at the outside door I gave it a shove and we walked out into the dark clear night. The temperature was pleasing and a warm breeze kissed my cheek. Only a few feet ahead of us was a gathering of about 40 people tightly packed against the rail overlooking the Colorado River. They were looking up at the star-filled sky. The bright stars seemed as numerous as grains of sand on the beach.

A large full moon hung in the southeastern sky. Its brightness dulled the view of the nearby stars. This entire scene was reflected in the shimmering waters of the Colorado. We took up a position behind a woman wearing a long white dress. She had gray hair and appeared to be in her late sixties. As we approached she turned and stated excitedly,

"Oh my, I think you missed them!"

"Missed what?" I responded.

She pointed up at the sky,

"There were about eight of them flying right about over there."

I responded by asking,

"Eight of what? What are you talking about?"

At this point she seemed a bit annoyed with my questions and barked quietly back at me,

"Eight craft. What did you think I was referring to?"

My wife and daughter heard her remark and gave me a quizzical look.

My mind began to race. I thought perhaps this woman and undoubtedly the others were having some natural visual aberration caused by twitching of the eye muscles when staring at a small bright object at night. I scanned the sky to see if I could also experience the same phenomenon. As I scanned the millions of stars I recalled the movie, *A Beautiful Mind,* and remembered the scene in which Russell Crowe's character pointed to the sky and asked his companion to pick a shape—an animal, anything, telling her he would point it out to her. She said "umbrella." He put his arm over hers and they extended them upwards towards the heavens and he drew it for her.

For some unknown reason I began to look for triangles. *Wow,* there were too many to count. I became transfixed on an equilateral triangle of stars located just to the left and slightly below the corona of the moon. Suddenly and without warning, the two bottom-most stars began to move. I took my eyes away, glanced at the ground and rubbed them with the back of my hand. To be on the safe side I took my glasses off for a quick inspection of the lenses. I replaced them and looked once again. Yes, unbelievably the very same stars were still moving. They moved downward and approached each other making a pair of slowly moving bright objects. I turned and surveyed the group of people we were with, including my wife and daughter. They were all eerily silent as they continued to visualize this amazing phenomenon. It was so quiet you could here a pin drop. I looked again at the moving stars. They were proceeding toward the bright left-hand side of the moon's corona. I thought to myself, "Could this be real? Is this really happening?"

Suddenly my thoughts were answered in the form of a thought-gram. One continuous message,

"Yes, you see us. We are real. Please believe what you are witnessing. Goodbye for now."

The paired objects proceeded directly into the corona of the moon and disappeared from view. The group of witnesses stood there silently without moving, as if in a state of enchantment or disbelief. Slowly, ever so slowly, they began to silently disperse. At that point my daughter turned to me and asked, "Daddy, will those guys who were flying those bright shiny planes come back and talk to us again?

I was shocked and assured her they would most probably someday return. I turned to my wife and asked her impression of what had just transpired. She responded by telling me she did not wish to talk about it.

We turned and began to walk away from the crowd. I felt a tug on my coat sleeve and there stood my friend Peter from the National UFO Reporting Center in Seattle, Washington. He excitedly said, "My God, Roger, did *you* see the same thing I saw? I think we should phone Art immediately"

He was referring to Art Bell, the famous radio talk show host of the late night program, *Coast to Coast*. I told him I did not have Art's number with me and asked if he had it. With that he whipped out his cell phone and began to dial the number. I asked my wife and daughter to go inside and wait for me, explaining I might have to be on a radio show for a short time. They seemed to understand the situation based on previous experiences and returned to the banquet room. At that point Peter looked dismayed, put the phone back into its holder and told me he couldn't get through to Art. I suggested we try again later or do a show at a later date.

Soon we were joined by several other UFO researchers who were also present at the conference. They expressed their interest in what we had just experienced. We explained what had just happened and they voiced their disappointment about not being there to see it. I consoled them, advising their presence was necessary at the award ceremony. After all, some of us had to be there to cheer on the award winners.

At that point all I really wanted to do was to get somewhere by myself and quietly ponder what had just transpired. I had always considered my life as being somewhat different and strange in comparison to my close friends. If anyone had told me 25 years ago I would be at a UFO conference in Nevada watching the stars move, I would have told them they were nuts. It seemed as if one synchronistic event after another brought me into this peculiar field of endeavor.

Only a few years ago I was an ordinary podiatric surgeon going about my business of professional private practice and raising a family. Suddenly, because of multiple synchronistic events I found myself at a UFO conference much like the present one, but at that time I was acting in the capacity of an investigative reporter. I had met a researcher who had been researching in the Alien Abduction field for many years. He had shown me X-rays of a foot which appeared to contain two foreign objects lodged in the big toe. The researcher touted these as being Alien Implants and I thought his statements to be utter nonsense. I challenged him by asking to have the objects removed and submitted for scientific scrutiny. He told me the abductee would most probably agree but she had no medical insurance or sufficient funds to cover the cost of a surgery. With that, I asked where the subject resided. He told me she lived in Texas. I looked him squarely in the eyes and stated in a of matter of fact tone, "Let me tell ya what. You get her to California and I'll do the surgery at no charge!!!"

With a wide-eyed expression on his face, he stared into my eyes and said, "Do you really mean that?"

"Yes, I certainly do!" I retorted.

With that he assured me he would be in contact again soon. As he had promised he not only made contact but the ultimate result was the first of two surgeries for removal of possible alien implants being performed on August 19, 1995. Since that time my surgical team has performed ten of these surgical procedures and the results have been mind-boggling.

Overnight I found myself deeply entrenched in this subject, as well as becoming a world renowned author who has appeared on numerous radio and TV broadcasts. I have traveled all over the world in an attempt to explain to audiences the reality of Alien Abductions, Alien Implants and UFOs. I have demonstrated the scientific evidence, the so-called "SMOKING GUN."

It was one thing to make these discoveries, but what to do with this evidence was a horse of another color. How could I spread the word? Who was ready to hear the truth? I discovered the public at large was not going to get it from mainstream media or from the scientific community. Perhaps this is why I choose to attend UFO conferences. At least here I am at home presenting my material to audiences who are interested in the phenomenon. Audiences who increase in size yearly. Maybe this is why my family and I were chosen to witness the stars move and able to hear the message from our non-earthly visitors.

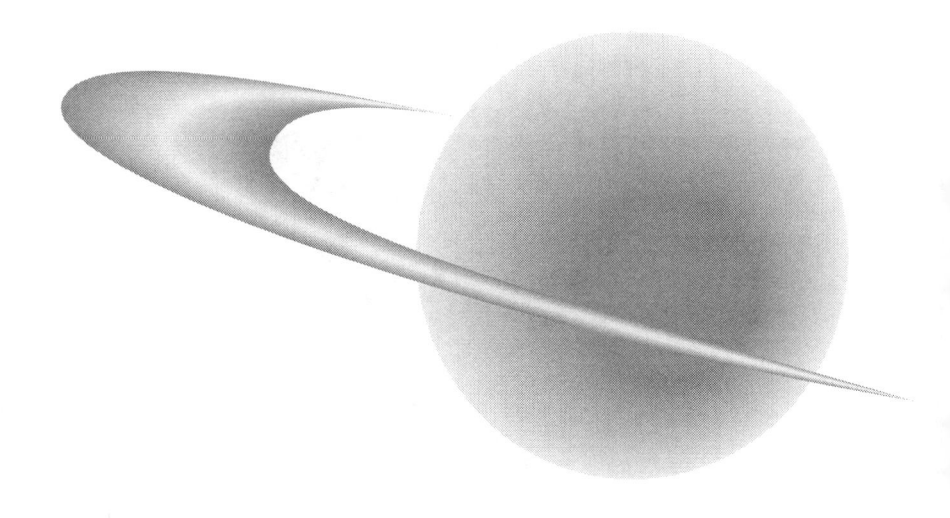

JOHN ALSTON

John Alston is an internationally known author, speaker, and performance strategist whose programs have lifted the spirits of millions of people worldwide. His consulting clients include Hewlett-Packard, Bank One, the FDIC, and the Ford Motor Co., among others. His books include: *Stuff Happens (and then you fix it!)* and *Goodness Must Be Taught: 29 Gifts of Wisdom from Papa's Letter.* Email: windjohn@aol.com

18 Lessons In a Legacy
by John Alston

Give your talents and skills freely...You never know when you're creating a memory!

When I was fifteen years old my parents, my sister and I went to the Seattle World's Fair in Washington State. We stayed with my great uncle (my grandfather's brother) who had a home overlooking Lake Washington. Early one morning I was admiring the view from his window and happened to see a waterskier skimming over the lake. I was intrigued and transfixed as I watched the skier's uncanny ability to glide over the smooth as glass early morning undisturbed lake water. Secretly I yearned for the thrill of doing something like this but never told anybody.

As I stood and watched, awed by the grace and style of these accomplished skiers, my great uncle sidled up next to me and asked, "What are you doing?" I turned toward him, and responded, pointing to the skiers, and said, "Look!" My uncle then asked, "Can you do that?" To which I responded, "No!" He said, "That's too bad."

We returned home to our daily summer routine. One day, soon after we returned, my mother received a phone call. A friend of my father, an attorney named Tom, said, "I just bought a boat and I'm taking some kids water-skiing for the weekend. Do you think Johnny would like to come along?"

When my mother asked me I said, "No, I have to clean my room. Are you serious, of course I want to go!" So they worked out the arrangements and Tom true to his word, arrived driving a motor home (a first experience for all of us) on a Friday evening. He picked me up and, along with three other young men, we were off to Indio, California, and the Salton sea. We arrived late in the evening, and registered at a local motel where the three boys and I got a room and threw one of the mattresses off the bed so we could sleep two to a mattress. It was 87 degrees that night. We had hamburgers, fries and shakes and easily fell asleep.

Early the next morning we went to get Tom's boat, "The Pink Lady" out of storage and launch it. I found myself at the lake waist deep in warm water with the other boys. Tom was up front in his brand new boat with his girlfriend, and his friend, who was to drive. To this day I remember the smell of the outboard motor fumes and water, a smell that continues to bring back the wonderful memory of this exhilarating day.

Tom looked back and asked, "Okay, who's first?" I immediately jumped at the opportunity. I nervously put on the skis as Tom threw me the towline. "Okay, keep your arms straight, your knees bent and stay behind the boat," he said as they started the engine. I took the towline handle and sat in the water with the ski tips up as instrumented. I said, "Hit it" and the boat took off. I was jerked up, flipped over flat on my face, and was dragged through the water. However, the only thing hurt was my pride.

This happened again and again. Five more attempts, each with the same outcome. It was after the fifth attempt that Tom then got out of the boat, waded back with another pair of skis for himself and an extra towline and sat down next to me in the water. "Now remember what I said. Keep your arms straight, your knees bent and stay behind the boat." We positioned ourselves for the next attempt. Ready, willing and able, we were both set.

Tom yelled out, "Hit it!" Again I attempted to get up, but this time Tom was skiing right next to me and actually reaching out with his hand to hold my upper arm straight. He kept saying right in my ear, again and again, actually yelling, "Keep your arms straight, arms straight!" as I tugged and tried to pull myself up. Again I fell. Again we tried it, but this time I locked it into my mind. I braced and locked my arms. Finally, I got it. I had locked it in my mind. "Arms straight. Knees bent" and I was—uh, well kinda—I was in sort of a squatting position, knees bent, arms straight, but I was on the surface of the water with Tom next to me still holding my arm and encouraging me to get into a more upright position, and I did. I got it. I kept my arms straight. I flexed my knees. Tom let go and there I was, alone and literally flying, skimming over the water as Tom yelled, "Stay behind the boat!"

Oh what a joy. I was now just like the guys I had watched on Lake Washington. I wished my uncle could see me. "Yes, uncle, I can do it." I dreamed about it. It was then that he must have realized what I had always wanted. Not only did I want to ski but I needed a teacher to pass on this skill. And a teacher had appeared.

Ten years later I bought a boat, and guess what? I got together some kids who wanted to learn how to water ski, took them out on the boat and told them the same things Tom had told me, "Okay, keep your arms straight, your knees bent and stay behind the boat." It was funny how the same scenario was repeated. The new kids all flopped and splashed, but some seemed to know exactly what to do.

I got out of the boat with an extra pair of skis and sat down next to each kid one at a time and said, "Okay, now remember, keep your arms straight, your knees bent, and stay behind the boat." I would take their arm, hold it out straight and together we would rise up to the surface. Everyone I ever took water-skiing learned how to do it and never forgot this great experience.

Proof? Ten year later, I get a call from one of these successful water-skiing kids, who was now grown. "Guess what?" she said, "I just bought a boat!"

This is a great example of developing your talents and giving them back to the world, but it is also an excellent metaphor of how to fix it when stuff happens in your life.

When you keep falling down: "Keep your arms straight, knees bent, and stay behind the boat." This means that in coping with the stuff life hands you, there are times when you have to be resolute and firm. You have to keep your arms straight. Then there are times when you have to be flexible enough to bend and flex when the sea of life becomes choppy. In order to remain upright, you have to remain behind what drives you, and what drives you also pulls you along. The drive in your life is your story, your vision for the future, and your values. Your values fuel what moves you forward.

Like water-skiing you can jump to the side from time to time and it is very smooth. But you can never get too far ahead of yourself. Remember, each of us needs other people to succeed. Tom learned to ski and taught others, and they learned and taught someone else. And that person continues the legacy.

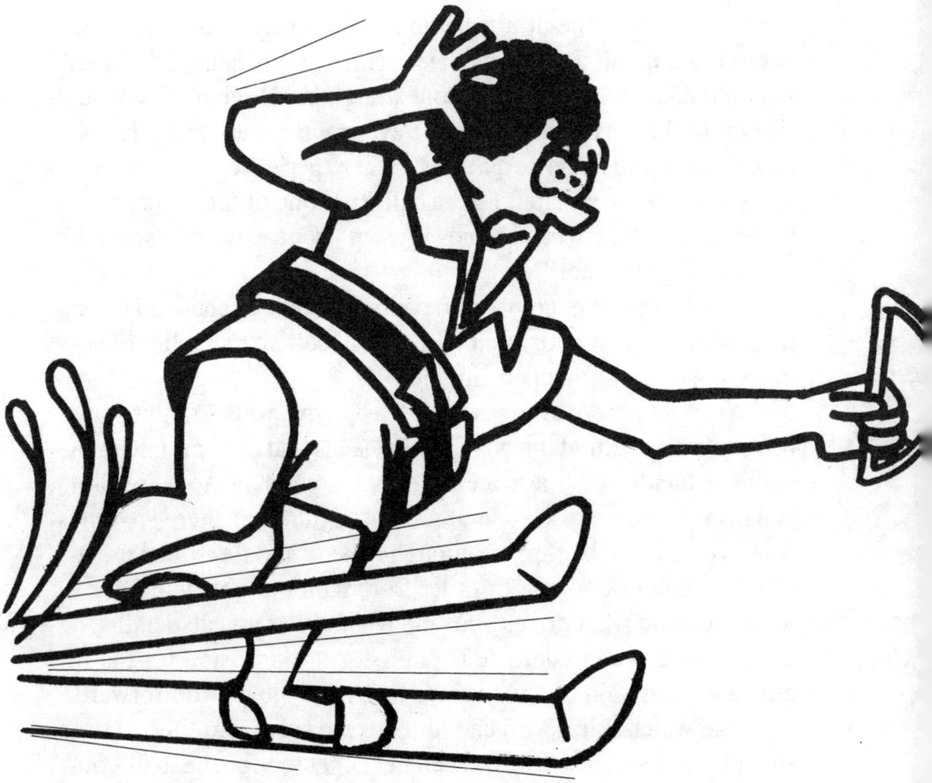

There are times in life, in fact most of the time, when in order to remain balanced you move with a stable entity, and a flexible one. It is like a spinning gyroscope. In order for it to remain upright there has to be an axis, a core that is firm and stable, solid and strong. Around the stable core, everything else is spinning. The two aspects working together enable it to remain upright and balanced.

In life you must do the same thing. Keeping your arms straight represents the firmness and steadiness required. Keeping your knees bent and flexing them allows the movement required. Staying behind the boat represents the pulling and the momentum of a forward vision, a mission, possessing a sense of where you want to go, what you want do, and ultimately what you want to become. And when you learn how to embrace all three, you'll find balance, remain upright and move forward.

DR. REX and LUCILLE INGRAHAM

A member of the University of Southern California School of Dentistry's Hall of Fame, Dr. Ingraham devoted his professional life to dental academics. He is the author of three textbooks and numerous articles in the field of Restorative Dentistry and has lectured and presented study courses on six continents.

He holds the title of Distinguished Professor Emeritus at the University of Southern California.

19 A Gift of Trust
by Rex Ingraham, D.D.S.

"Rich is not how much you have, or where you are going, or even what you are. Rich is who you have beside you."

Lucille and I have been married since 1963. We are now in our eighties, very happy, and are still deeply in love. On the next page is an acronym for easily remembering the blueprint for building a solid and supportive relationship which has worked for us.

Our two greatest gifts from God are our freedom and life itself. Next comes the gift of love and eternal companionship. The key that opens this box of gifts is called Trust.

Dr. Pam Gefke has said, "Every game has ground rules for civilized, fair play. So why not marriage? Heaven knows, wherever two people are gathered, sooner or later they'll find reasons for conflict."

She also said, "What could make you feel more secure in your marriage, as you work to resolve your disagreements, than to decide on some rules to live by? Wouldn't it be reassuring to have a plan for accomplishing a win/win resolution for settling differences as they occur?"

Difficult situations and problems come like hormones during puberty—often painful and confusing, but necessary for our growth. Victories come when we learn to handle each situation effectively. As children we scream and argue to solve problems. If that remains your only option as an adult, then marriage is a poor choice. Those who think that shouting nasty, unkind words at each other solves anything must also believe that the only way to turn out the lights is with a baseball bat.

The following seven principles form the basis for a relationship that is **L - A - S - T - I - N - G** in both friendships *and* marriages:

L aughter and Fun—
It's nearly impossible for anyone to both laugh and argue at the same time. The late Ruth Hale, a playwright and a legend in American community theater, had a favorite way of creating ideas for her plays. She would turn her family's disagreements and conflicts into stage comedy. When the problem was finally resolved and everyone was laughing about it, she made sure the theater audiences had *their* chance to laugh also.

Ruth proved over the years that beneath the worst confrontations lurked a lesson, a laugh, the punchline of a joke, or a phrase worthy of repeating. Her formula or equation for comedy was:
Disaster plus time equals humor.

If you're tired, burnt-out, sickly...a sense of humor leaves you quickly. To laugh or smile is such a strain...but if you don't, you're just a pain!

A ffection—
The enjoyment of touching or stroking is found at all levels of life. Petting the noses of dolphins at the aquarium, or the fur on your dog or cat, creates a mutually satisfying feeling.

Assurance, and frequent *re*assurance, is needed for even the most secure among us. We all like to know we're accepted. Isolation is not the normal condition of a happy, well-adjusted person, and can lead to separation among friends and spouses. To know on a daily basis that nothing has changed between the two of you, and that your relationship is getting even better, is one of the essentials to a happy disposition.

A spontaneous kiss, a squeeze of the hand, a hug for no reason, a compliment or expression of appreciation, or a love- note are valued more than we'll ever know. Avoidance of criticism, teasing, and threats also assures closeness.

S imilar Backgrounds and Interests—
Marriages between those who have very different cultural experiences and interests have less of a chance to be successful. In our case we both came from rural areas with a high level of family-

encouraged morality and values. Our religious beliefs and ideals were similar, which statistically bodes well for future compatibility. We have common interests in many exciting activities, among them skiing, fishing, and football.

T eachable—

A life filled with excitement requires an attitude that anything is possible. Each new day holds a promise if you're aware and prepared for it. Lifelong learning—whether it be formal, through reading, or the need to do research for writing assignments—is essential for an active mind. Often as the mind goes, so goes the body.

I ntelligent Choices—

Obtain as much education each day as possible, be of service to others, avoid abusing your body, and take only the chances you can handle without anxiety. Calmly coping with unavoidable problems will assure anyone a better chance at marital success.

N utrition and Exercise—

The value of maintaining mobility and staying in condition is essential to a long, productive, active and happy life. Lack of exercise or attention to a proper diet is one of the fastest way to destroy one's mind, body, marriage, career and longevity.

G oal-Setting—

Dreams and ambitions need not be abandoned as you get older. Perseverance and the focus on worthwhile objectives help you to stay at the highest level of your potential.

ERNEST LEWIS (Weckbaugh)

Below:
E R N I E and friends Alfalfa (left) and Spanky (right) in the *Our Gang Comedies* (1937 to 1941)

Ernie Weckbaugh began his "professional" life as an actor at the age of five (*Little Rascals/Our Gang Comedies*). An illustrator in the Air Force during the Korean War, he worked as an artist in aerospace and advertising while earning his degree. He married Patty Palmer (1960) and they became business partners (Casa Graphics, Inc.) in 1975.

He is the co-author of *Book Blitz, Getting Your Book in the News*, and has helped countless self-publishing authors produce their books. As president of Book Publicists of Southern California, he created the IRWIN Awards and the *Chopped Liver* anthologies to encourage writer/publicists to develop their careers through publishing.

20 Bombs Bursting In Air
by Ernest Lewis
(Weckbaugh)

When I see a young person staring into space, doodling intently, muttering or talking to himself, I see a kindred spirit. Any member of my family will tell you that most of the time as a youth my mind was "absent." I would sit for hours in the top of the back yard peach tree and stare off into the sky. I was known for locking myself into the only bathroom of our tiny home for hours to study the dictionary. Of all the books in the house, this was my favorite. It never told me what to see or feel like other books did. With one word as a starting point, I could create my own stories and fantasies.

Each new word unlocked a chamber of my private world. While the rest of the family took turns pounding on the bathroom door, I trained myself to ignore such distractions, and it was there that I learned the valuable art of concentration. To this day my brother and sister can't understand how I come up with ideas. They compare it to drawing water from an empty well.

I used to fill every blank sheet of paper I could find from top to bottom with little drawings. My mother could never find anything to write on. While walking home from school, I would carry on a two-sided, animated conversation—out loud. When I recently heard of a book titled *What to Say When You Talk to Yourself* by Shad Helmstetter, I finally realized I was not alone in having my own little world.

Most people have a colorful relative or two. I had them by the carloads. Relatives from both sides of our family had a habit of dropping in, unexpectedly, from either Nebraska or Colorado, even Panama. I loved the excitement and the funny stories that were passed around, the presents and the silver dollars they gave us. However, I noticed my mother was never very happy about them coming. She was expected to prepare big meals for them for a week, and somehow fit them all in our three bedrooms. They never said a word about going to a hotel. I noticed she began picking up my habit of talking to herself.

Relatives were assigned several to a room, where my older, teen-aged brother and sister and I had already gone. I listened from my room to the frequent outbursts of laughter for an hour or so, followed by movement and hushed voices in the hall as they prepared to retire. The two assigned to my room shuffled in quietly apologizing, smelling of cigars and beer, running into lamps and chairs in the dark. The novelty of these adults playing *Three Stooges* with the unseen furniture made falling asleep difficult.

However, *they* had no problem falling asleep—*soundly!* Suddenly I was startled and terrified by their deafening snores. I realized I was faced with this long-playing chorus without hope of sleep for the next seven hours. It was going to be a test of my sanity to rival any horror movie. Somehow I had to think my way through it.

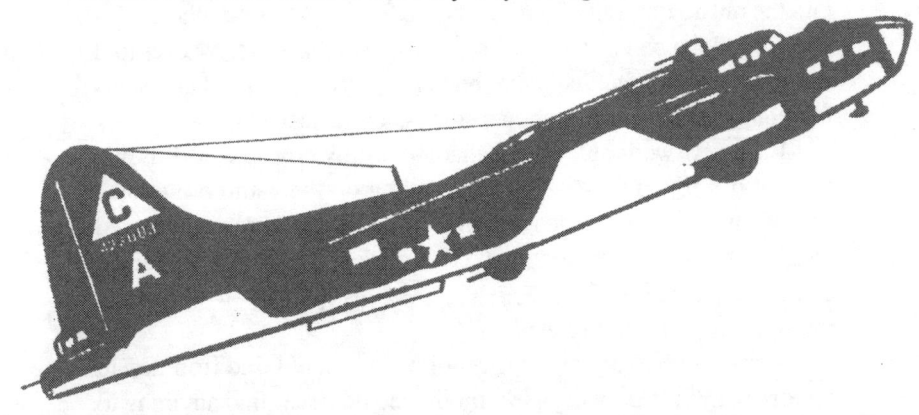

I slowly drifted off—not into sleep, but into fantasy. It was about the time America was entering World War II. With my pillow as my parachute and backrest, I sat at the controls of my fully loaded B-17 bomber somewhere in the night sky over Germany. As I pulled on my toy goggles, I realized I was surrounded by the Germans (these were my father's relatives). But they also happened to be loyal Americans, and I was counting on them that night. On my left, at 10 o'clock high, Uncle Eugene pierced the darkness with his nasal artillery. I had little to fear, though, with the steady drone of my Pratt & Whitney engines (it was really Uncle Eugene and Aunt Lydia, and a more faithful drone you couldn't wish for).

It seemed like an eternity (these missions were always longer than anticipated), but the constant hum of the rest of the squadron (in the adjoining bedrooms) gave me comfort and encouragement.

At last we reached our target area. Rapidly we prepared the bombs for release. At the precise moment, right on cue, Aunt Lydia began making a whistling sound just after the bombs were released. I *knew* that I could count on her. Thirty-thousand feet below I began to hear the blockbusters exploding on target. I almost cheered out loud.

I wasn't worried about the long flight home. Our giant engines still pulsed away with only an occasional cough, sputter or wheeze. I can still remember the faint light on the horizon through the windows. We landed at dawn.

I felt strangely victorious at breakfast that morning. I had survived the night without losing my mind, and I'd had an exciting and memorable adventure. In the years that followed, my imagination came to my rescue on many occasions. I began to believe I could do, or be, whatever I wished through the magic of creativity.

DR. GRAY and JOANNE BERG

Grey and Joanne Berg, both retired, give more than a thousand volunteer hours apiece each year at their local sheriff's station; their dog is in a Pet Assisted Therapy (PAT) program; they devote time to the Assistance League; and spend two mornings a week at a local elementary school in a reading enrichment program.

21 From "The Wall" to "Ground Zero"

by Gray Berg, D.D.S., and Joanne Berg

Some of our most rewarding adventures have been spontaneous, evolving from national and international circumstances. In January of 1990, my wife Joanne came home from work and said she'd just heard that the Berlin Wall was being torn down. She proposed we should see it before it was completely demolished and began to make flight reservations, adjust work schedules and arrange a "dog-sitter" for our two Great Danes. Our passports are always on hand and we have a small bag always packed with toiletries and a change of clothes. This time she even persuaded our friend Rosemary Hook to accompany us. Before any of us had time to think, we were on a plane to Berlin.

Stopping only to register at our hotel, we hopped a bus for the short ride to the wall. It was an amazing sight, people milling about on the streets and on top of the wall. In contrast to the wild celebrations we had seen on television before we left, there was a very somber atmosphere now, coupled with a determination to destroy this symbol of separation of families and political ideology. And through the ever enlarging holes in the wall we could see the East German soldiers with guns in their hands and a look of bewilderment and fascination on their faces. They were too young to have ever known Berlin before the wall was put up. German families walked along the wall and it was obvious they were talking very seriously to their young children about this momentous occasion in their lives. Some were so young they'll never actually remember the day, but their parents were filming it as an historic moment.

A little farther on from the Brandenburg Gate and the Reichstag building we came upon an area marked with dozens of simple wooden crosses. They represented the many who had been killed trying to escape from East Germany. An English-speaking Berliner explained that many more people had been killed than the number of crosses indicated, but the crosses were more symbolic than numerically accurate.

I had planned to buy a hammer and chisel from a hardware store to break out our own piece of the wall, but as I saw what difficulty other "chippers" were having, we went to Plan "B." We found a group from a hospital for the indigent who were making good progress with sledge hammers. They had a sign that read, "Take as much as you want, donate as much as you wish!" (I was able to roughly translate this.) We made a donation and took what turned out to be 20 pounds of the wall. On our return to the states we shared this with friends and relatives, and even the tiniest chips were taken by our friend Sister Clarice who used them as projects for students in schools where she taught.

After a trip the next day to the site of Hitler's bunker, which was in an area which had been completely leveled with only a slight rise in the ground to indicate where the bunker had been, we left for Munich. We took a very heart-wrenching trip to the infamous Dachau concentration camp and a drive by Lechfeld Air Base where I had been stationed just after the end of World War II. It had been returned to German control some years ago and we weren't able to enter the base, but it was a nostalgic drive in any event. From the Munich area we drove up the Romantic Road to Rothenburg, an ancient walled city. We stayed in a very old inn with no elevators. When the bellman was struggling up the stairs with Joanne's suitcase, now weighing the extra 20 pounds, I explained that it contained a piece of the Berlin Wall, to which the bellman replied, "Then I am honored to be carrying it!"

It was a trip I probably wouldn't have initiated but one of the most amazing trips we've ever taken. Everywhere there was this great feeling of euphoria, joy at being reunited with relatives, and such optimism for the future. In the famous Hofbrau in Munich, the beer was being drunk and toasts to the future being made long into each night.

* * *

On September 11, 2001, we were at a family reunion in eastern Ohio, just a few miles from where Flight 94 crashed. By the end of the week we made the decision to drive home to California when it seemed clear we might spend more time waiting in airports than it would take to drive. That four-day trip showed us the greatest display of patriotism we've seen since World War II. Buildings, trucks, homes, highway overpasses and hundreds of cars flew flags or banners with the "we will never forget" and "God bless America" themes. Whether that experience heightened our desire to provide "hands on" help to New York I'm not sure, but two months later Joanne and I were on our way to New York, again within days of making the decision to go. We hadn't been able to make any specific contacts but were advised by some of our local firefighters who had just returned from New York that Pier 94 was where all the work was going on.

As soon as we arrived we took a cab to Pier 94 and approached the secured site where we talked to a Federal Emergency Management Authority (FEMA) representative standing at the barricades. We told him we were in New York for a week and would like to help in some way. He took us inside, where we went through airport-type security scanners, signed us in and introduced us to an official with a group called "Safe Horizons." Their function was to provide immediate financial help to displaced residents, workers or families of victims. We spent the first few hours observing other interviewers and then began interviewing applicants ourselves. The stories were bone-chilling and heartbreaking, with people in apartments near the trade centers telling us of body parts and airplane parts in their apartments, separation from other family members, loss of businesses, etc. Each day we left Safe Horizons feeling emotionally exhausted but ready nevertheless to come back the next day to do it again.

Pier 94 itself was an unbelievable hub of activity, with every possible agency victims might need to contact under one roof. There was crisis counseling, Salvation Army, Red Cross, Unemployment Insurance agencies, legal services, notary services, clergy, therapy dogs, food stamps, and more. Applicants were initially screened as they entered the facility and given a folder with a sheet listing all the agencies in the building. Those who might assist a particular applicant were checked on the sheet and the applicant could go from agency to agency all under one roof to get whatever assistance was needed. It was mind-boggling to realize the organizational skills needed to operate such a facility. What we learned was that companies clamored to loan computers, copiers, food, employees, anything to help. There was one wall extending the full length of the building covered with posters of missing relatives, letters from families of victims with messages of love and loss, Teddy Bears sent from children in Oklahoma City, flowers, mementos, etc. It was a wall of grief and agony but also resolve to stand together and go on.

This was truly one of our most rewarding trips—it was not a fun and games trip, but each day we felt we'd done something worthwhile and had directly helped, if only in an infinitesimal way.

JANIE LEE

22 Of Horses and Bathtubs
by Janie Lee

Once in a while you hear of great teachers, and what they do to motivate their students. They become "Teacher of the Year." They win the "Crystal Apple" awards. They are recognized and honored throughout the school district.

Two of my sons were each blessed to have instructors like this.

In 1973 there was a nationwide shortage of gasoline due to our unfortunate dependence on foreign oil, and the alleged attempt on the part of the OPEC nations to cripple our transportation system, and to control us where it hurts on the most personal level. Whatever the reason, many of us still remember it well. You could fill your tank only on an every other day schedule depending on the last number of your license plate, either odd or even. If it was an even numbered day, like January 2, only those with the last numbers 2, 4, 6, 8, or 0 could line up around the block at the local gas station and, in a few hours, you might have the chance to buy enough gas to get to work.

Some people reacted in a most creative way. My son Douglas' teacher decided, since she owned a horse, to express her irritation with the system by riding it to school. She apparently had no idea the impact it would have on her students.

Well, her little mare became the hit of the school. So she decided to use it a variety of ways. As a lesson plan, it became a visual aid for teaching animal anatomy; she wrote word problems in arithmetic with the horse involved where the students had to add, subtract, etc., as the horse performed certain tasks, traveling certain distances, carrying so much weight, etc.; as a reward, those who did their homework on time joined the list of those who could ride the pony around the school grounds, the coolest privilege imaginable. Those who didn't do their work had to join the list of those who washed and groomed the horse. This was not an unpleasant chore, it just told everyone who was watching that you were the "dunce for a day."

The presence of this very handsome beast made celebrities out of her students, the envy of their schoolmates. The test scores and achievement level of her pupils rose dramatically. Her rapport with faculty couldn't have been higher. When she had to give up horseback riding to school and return to driving an ordinary car as an ordinary teacher, it was a sad day indeed.

Mustang
very low mileage

My other son, Darryl, had an equally innovative experience in his classroom. His teacher didn't use a national event or a thousand pound pet to gain their attention. He just used a simple *bathtub!* For some inexplicable reason, it was considered by all of his students to be a great honor to spend the day propped up on pillows in this empty bathtub as a result of having the highest grade on the last test, turning in the best paper, having perfect attendance, etc. They were treated with great deference, waited on, and given special privileges since it wasn't necessary for them to leave the tub, unless they wanted to or *had* to.

This bathtub, like the horse, put the class under the complete control of the teacher, and in a way the students loved and even fought for the privilege. Again, the reputation for doing these things quickly spread throughout the school, and the upcoming students couldn't wait to get promoted in order to have the experience. In school systems struggling with students who can't do the necessary work year in and year out, sometimes it's creative teachers doing simple things combined with a little bit of imagination that can make all the difference.

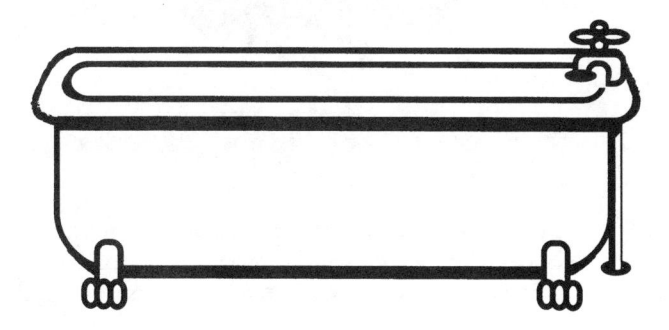

DOTTIE WALTERS

Dottie Walters, CSP, is an international speaker, author, and consultant. She is the publisher/editor: of *Sharing Ideas* magazine, a world renowned publication for professional speakers, meeting planners and speakers' bureau owners. Dottie is president of her own Walters International Speakers Bureau, and is the publisher of the International Directory of Speakers Bureaus. She is also the founder of the International Association of Speakers Bureau Owners, and is proud to be a member of the Book Publicists of Southern California.

www.walters-intl.com. Phone (626) 335-8069
or email: dottie@walters-intl.com.

23 Opportunity Is Always Located *"At Hand"*
by Dottie Walters, CSP

I went to hear the very famous speaker and author Dr. Norman Vincent Peale. I went up to him after his presentation and handed him my new business card. What happened because of that moment changed my life and sent me all over the world! Here is how it happened:

The economy after World War II caused many people to be laid off work. My sweetheart, Bob Walters, returned after four years with the Marine Corps in the South Pacific. He was decorated for bravery after he went back into the water at Tarawa under enemy machine gun fire to rescue wounded men in his platoon. As soon as Bob got back to Southern California we were married, bought a GI-financed tract home, a dry-cleaning franchise, and had two beautiful babies. *Then the economy got worse!*

No one was using any dry cleaning. When Bob came home one night after knocking on doors all day asking for dry-cleaning orders, he sat and put his head in his hands. I had never seen him so down. He said he did not know where he would be able to get the money for our house payment. I told him I had an idea. If he could give me a couple of weeks, I thought I could help. I could see that he didn't believe there was anything I could do with two babies and no car. He had to take our old car to the dry-cleaning store each day. What *could* I do to help?

My father had abandoned my mother and me just as I was about to go to high school. I worked at many different jobs, giving my mother my checks during those four high school years. But then a wonderful thing happened. My English teacher asked the class to each choose a character from Charles Dickens' book *A Tale of Two Cities* and write about him. We were to write about where the character came from, and what happened to the character next?

She read my story aloud to the class!

My heart sailed around the room that day. Then my English teacher announced that I would be the Advertising Manager & Feature Editor for the Alhambra High *Moor*, our school newspaper, for the new term. I was thrilled!

I sold the ads on my lunch hour. However, the only time I had to work on my feature ideas was at night. The bakery I worked in was very quiet the last two hours of my eight hour shift. Very few customers came in from 10 p.m. until midnight when my Mom came to pick me up. I wrote on the clean sides of partially soiled bakery bags after I scrubbed the shelves, floors and the pans that held the bakery products.

Then the next morning I took my ad copy and articles into my journalism class. My teacher laughed saying she had never had a journalism student turn in stories and ads on bakery bags before!

One of my ideas was a comedy Advice to the Lovelorn column by a fictional "Professor O.G. Whataline!" Everyone loved it, and no one guessed who wrote it (me). Another idea was a Shoppers' Column with paragraphs about different stores in town. Each merchant paid to appear in that column, which I wrote. I sold the column spots as I sold the display ads to the same businesses.

The Shoppers' Column was my idea solution to pay our house payment. I would write a Shoppers' Column right there in our chicken ranching town of Baldwin Park, California, for the weekly newspaper, *The Baldwin Park Bulletin*. Then it hit me. I had no typewriter, no car, nor even any typing paper.

What would I do with my two small children when I tried to sell the Shoppers' Column spaces? I had only one pair of shoes, and the soles were almost worn out. There were very few sidewalks in Baldwin Park. On the day my father left us he had answered my mother's question about my going to college in a voice so loud all the neighbors could hear him – *She does not need any college!* he yelled, because I was *"too dumb to be worth educating."*

My reaction was to turn to the public library where I read biographies of people of accomplishment and achievement. I felt so close to them as I read about their dreams and how they overcame problems that I could hear their voices! Each famous person became my *"Friend of the Mind."*

Many years later, as I told this story about the voices in the books, a lady in my audience called out "How dare you say those authors wrote their books for you! Most of them wrote their books long before you were born!"

I answered her this way: "If they did not write them for my yearning, listening heart—who did they write them for?" My audience was silent a minute and then gave me a standing ovation.

So I grabbed a pencil and made a list of what I needed to write a Shoppers' Column for *The Baldwin Park Bulletin*. Each item needed a solution.

1. A typewriter.
2. Typing paper.

3. **A way to take the children with me** as I walked to town to sell my Shoppers' Column to the merchants.
4. My shoes were almost worn out. How could I fix them so that I could walk the two miles to town on the rocky streets with no sidewalks?

Since I did not have any of these things, my heart sank. Then I remembered reading about Albert Einstein. In the book about him at the Baldwin Park Library, he said to me: "Stop fussing about problems, Dottie! *INSTEAD—concentrate on SOLUTIONS!*"

The minute the word "SOLUTIONS" popped up on the screen of my mind I thought of my neighbor who had an old typewriter. I ran next door to her house and asked if I might borrow it for a couple of weeks. She was glad to loan it to me, and handed me a whole ream of typing paper! A whole REAM! I was so glad to see that ream of paper I could hardly hold back my tears of appreciation.

After I wrote a sample column based on the ads in the sample newspaper the *Bulletin* had thrown on my front porch, I got our old baby stroller out of the garage and tried to put both of our children into it. However I quickly saw that they no longer could both fit on the one seat. They had grown! Mr. Einstein called out to me again, "Solutions! SOLUTIONS!"

I ran into the bedroom and pulled the pillows off our bed. Then I grabbed my clothesline rope and tied the pillows on the back of the stroller to make a 2nd seat. I cut pieces from a cardboard carton from the grocery store to fit my shoes. I made several extra sets. I put the first set in my shoes, the rest into my purse.

Off we went!

The stroller wheel came off several times, but I just took off my shoe and let that old wheel have it with the heel!

When we reached town and found the newspaper office, I saw on the door a big sign "NO HELP WANTED!" My heart hit the sidewalk, but my good friend of the mind Ben Franklin (a journalist, too) whispered in my ear: "Dottie, they do not have any money to hire you, so do not ask for a job. Instead, become a customer for them! Buy their ad space at wholesale and sell it at retail. That way you will not hurt the newspaper's rates, and I promise you, you will have the money for your house payment in 2 weeks."

The publisher let me have the first two columns on credit, bless his heart! The merchants of Baldwin Park loved my Shoppers' Column, and Ben Franklin's prediction came true. I was able to pay that first house payment, and never missed one from then on.

Then my girl friend bought two tickets for the Pasadena Civic Auditorium where Dr. Norman Vincent Peale was to speak. He was coming all the way from New York. She bought my ticket as a gift. I was so excited. I had read every book at the Baldwin Park Library about advertising, sales and journalism. And, I had read Dr. Peale's *The Power of Positive Thinking*. He was like a great friend cheering me on each time I picked up his books.

My girl friend was in a hurry to leave after Dr. Peale's presentation, but I insisted on waiting in line to meet him in person to thank him for writing his book—for me! I had just managed to have my first business cards printed, so I pulled one out of my purse and held it out to him when it was my turn in line. He not only took it from me, he said "Tell me about it." I quickly told him about my "Friends of the Mind" and my Shoppers' Column and how I was now able to make the house payment. He had the kindest face I have ever seen. I held my breath wondering if he would hand my card back to me. But no! He put it in his inside coat pocket. I thought, "He didn't throw me away!"

Then a week later Dr. Peale called me on the phone and asked if he could send one of the interviewers for his **Guideposts Magazine** to see me so that they could publish a story about me. They wanted to title it "What Can One Housewife Do?"

The interviewer came to see us, and at the end of her questions she asked me what else I was working on. I told her that I had read every book at our library by Dr. Peale, and also everything about advertising and sales. But I noticed that there was no book *by* a woman, or *for* women in sales. The librarian tried to order books for me by *women* on these subjects from the county and state libraries, but there were none. Suddenly, I told her, in my mind, I saw my book on an empty library shelf! The title: *Never Underestimate the Selling Power of a Woman*.

Then two weeks later Dr. Peale called me again! He said that he had been telling his audiences my story! He said they all wanted to buy my book but could not find it. He asked me who my publisher was. I had to tell him that 18 publishers had turned down my manuscript because they all agreed there were no women in sales in the United States.

Dr. Peale told me, "Dottie, tomorrow I have an appointment to talk to my publisher, Prentice Hall. I will take some of the copies of our *Guideposts* magazine that featured your story and give them to my editor."

It was two days later that Prentice Hall called and asked for my manuscript! All the big Direct Sales companies were starting up: Amway, Mary Kay Cosmetics, Tupperware, and many more. The Great American Spirit of Enterprise was alive and well! Then Prentice Hall called to tell me that Tupperware planned to buy out the entire first edition of my *Never Underestimate the Selling Power of a Woman*. That led to my speaking to many Tupperware conventions and then other direct sales companies.

Then one day Prentice Hall called to tell me they had arranged for me to be on the popular TV show "What's My Line." My husband and I would be flown to New York. Neither of us had ever been there before. What a thrilling trip! One of the things I wanted to do was to take the ship ride around the harbor so that I could see the Statue of Liberty as it must have looked to my grandfather as he sailed into New York.

None of the stars on the TV show guessed that the country girl from the chicken ranching town of Baldwin Park could possibly be the author of the first book in the whole world for women in sales. (Until that moment I did not realize it was the first. I thought there must be other books on the subject, but I just hadn't found them yet.)

The TV show had chosen two women to appear with me who looked something like me, about the same age, coloring, and height. The first was from Brooklyn. She had a heavy New York accent and sold girdles in a bargain basement. The second, a very refined lady, wore little white gloves, and ran a young ladies' "finishing school" in the South. The third person was me, the young housewife from the chicken ranching town in the West.

We three each had to answer the same questions. One was "Who was the first American Advertising and Publicity man?" The other women gave names of well known people in those fields. When it was my turn, I said my great "Friend of the Mind," Benjamin

Franklin. I won! So we were able to bring back the prize money, and the Baldwin Park Chamber of Commerce held a "Welcome Home Dottie" banquet in my honor.

If you are feeling left behind, or discouraged, may I suggest that you go to the library and meet my "Friends of the Mind." They are the greatest thinkers and doers in the world, just waiting for you in their books. Please tell them Dottie sends her love and heartfelt appreciation. Solving the problem of our house payment led me to speak all over the world, open more businesses that tie into the world of paid speaking, write other books, publish a big magazine about the world of paid speaking. And, most of all, to have the great pleasure of people coming up to me carrying one of my books, all dog-eared and marked up, and USED WELL, asking me to autograph it for them. I always tell them as I gladly do so, *"I wrote it for you."*

PATTY PALMER
(Weckbaugh)

Patty Palmer Weckbaugh was born in Glendale, California. A graduate of Occidental College in education, she taught elementary school and acted in college and little theater plays before becoming business partners with her husband, Ernie, in their advertising and book production business.

24 The Murder Mystery that Killed the Audience
by Patty Palmer
(Weckbaugh)

It was a play never to be forgotten, certainly by no one in the cast or audience. It is still remembered some 45 years later as an example for those who think that perfection is necessary for theatrical success.

I had just graduated from Glendale City College and had started my junior year at Occidental College. Although an education major, I had nonetheless been in every play during my junior college years, and my fascination with acting transferred—when I did—to Occidental's four-year elementary education program.

College drama departments and little theaters perform a wide variety of plays, most of them comedies. I had performed in *The Man Who Came to Dinner*, *House Party*, *Kind Lady*, and *Greensleeves Magic* (a children's theatre production) while in junior college; *Dear Ruth* at the Glendale Center Theatre; *Country Girl* with the Foothill Curtain Raisers; and a song and dance olio act between scenes of a melodrama. But I always looked forward to the opportunity of being in a real mystery/drama.

When I found out through friends in the drama department at Occidental that a Play Mill production of a Patrick Hamilton play named *Angel Street*, the stage version of the Ingrid Bergman/Charles Boyer classic movie *Gaslight*, had been performed the previous year I was quite excited to know more. The Play Mill Theater in the basement of the campus theatre building known as Thorne Hall was intended for student productions for directing and acting finals, and held audiences of about 75. I became friends with many of the very talented members of the drama department, who related the story of this "outstanding" production. Many of my new friends had been in the cast that had created this legend on campus.

Angel Street was a very serious drama, with deep psychological issues dealing with induced insanity and a carefully planned plot to drive the female lead out of her mind. The goal of the play was to draw the mystery-loving audience into the intrigue by slowly building tension and suspense in a hushed auditorium.

The actor who related the story to me had played the Charles Boyer character. He insisted on wearing a glued-on mustache and sideburns applied with eyebrow pencil in order to appear properly sinister. Unfortunately, the mustache came unstuck on one side of his upper lip, perhaps due to nervous perspiration. The Bergman character was named Bella, and each time he yelled "*Bella!*" which he did frequently, the right side of his prop mustache blew forward. Always in character, he maintained his composure as the audience began to snicker.

Later on in the scene, Bella gave him a big hug and one of the black, painted-on sideburns transferred to her cheek. Whenever she turned that side of her face to the audience, the laughter surged.

Then the maid brought in a tray of tea cups and saucers. She inadvertently placed it precariously on the edge of the coffee table, half on and half off. The shaky floor of the stage and the action of the actors rushing back and forth rattled and teetered the tray with every move. The audience gasped every time it tipped. She kept loading and removing full and empty cups, first on the table side, then on the off-side of the tray. The audience sat on the edge of their seats. They talked and chuckled among themselves with their eyes glued on the shaking tray, breathlessly waiting for it to fall, which it never did.

Another performer, handsome and with a beautifully dramatic voice, had become known for never being able to memorize the volume of words needed for major parts. Nevertheless, he was cast as one of the leads. He solved his problem by typing out his lines and taping them onto props, the furniture, on his left and right sleeves, writing them on his hands, or inside his hat.

With great, characteristic flair, he strode confidently from the wings and delivered one line after another flawlessly. As his part continued, however, he slowly began to lose his poise as he searched the stage furniture and props for his next line. He completely lost track of where his lines were and finally just started using the script he had in his pocket, much to the added amusement of the audience.

At one point he needed to open a locked drawer. Trying to hold a flashlight in the semi-darkness with one hand, the key in the other, he had no hand to hold the script. His desperate fussing and fumbling was not lost on the audience, who by that time was convinced this was one of the best comedy/melodramas they'd ever seen.

With the blowing of the mustache with each *"Bella;"* the tray of cups rocking but never tumbling; and an actor hunting frantically all over the stage for his next line—the audience laughter grew from the opening to the final curtain, much to the surprise and confusion of the poor director. He had thought, through all of the rehearsals, that this was a mystery/drama. From where he stood backstage, when the audience was supposed to gasp with horror, instead he heard them roaring with laughter. Only the players and the audience knew why, and they would never tell him.

Many of the members of that cast went on to careers in the theatre or to teach drama. I'm sure they've all learned and passed on an important lesson—sometimes chaos, minor disasters, accidents, and imperfections can create memorable moments in the theatre and, incidently, some of the most delightful entertainment. They shouldn't be taken too seriously. It often makes life more interesting.

ELLSWORTH
PLUMSTEAD

GRANDPA PLUM
In one of his many characterizations

ELIZABETH THOMPSON
His granddaughter Elizabeth and
both great-granddaughters
Victoria and Hillary
also became actors

ELIZABETH
also in character as
"Not just another pretty face"

25 The Character Man
by Elizabeth Thompson

When I was small, he was our most mysterious grandparent. Most of the time he was away on the road. Then the announcement would come that Grandpa Plum was coming home, and excitement and anticipation took over! When he finally arrived, we would all look forward to his favorite trick to entertain us—balancing a broom handle on his nose and, at the same time, juggling three oranges.

His name was Ellsworth Plumstead, and for many years he toured with the Chautauqua as an actor, a form of early vaudeville. He traveled with the Redpath Chautauqua throughout every state and five Canadian provinces. He entertained at a time when there were no microphones or speakers, and "good acoustics" were unheard of in those old brown fabric tents. He was known as a "character man" and had developed a larger-than-life persona, a voice to be heard by thousands, and a wide range of parts to play—a virtual one-man repertory theater.

A typical playbill poster (circa 1906), seen throughout North America:

> **"The Wandering Raggedy Man"**
> **Ellsworth Plumstead**
> ENTERTAINER
> In Medley Programmes of
> *Songs, Stories, Costume Selections*
> *and Character Delineations*
> from the Poems and Prose of Today

A review from the *Inter-Mountain Republican*, Salt Lake City:
Entertained by Plumstead—It was an appreciative audience that listened to the quaint humor and droll wit of Ellsworth Plumstead for more than two hours last night. Mr. Plumstead appeared in the Star lecture course series and furnished one of the most pleasant evenings thus far. Perhaps the best effort of the entertainer was in the characterization of the young author—the young fellow with nothing but his poetic talent to carry him through the whirl of busy New York, who finally lands on the sixth floor of a tenement building, without a cent to his name, before the first check is received. The portrayal furnishes about the best subject for the peculiar talent of Mr. Plumstead.

From time to time he would return to our home in Michigan with exotic objects collected from each of his many appearances, such as Indian arrowheads, pottery and little native dolls for each of us.

Born during the Civil War in 1863, his career peaked at the turn of the century. He dressed and bore himself with style. He had that rich actor's speaking voice as well as a trained singing voice. He both embarrassed and intrigued us with his habit of intoning musical scales—do, mi, sol, do, mi, do—as he went about the house.

He wasn't used to being with little children. I never thought he really saw me during those early days. But all of us received his juicy, though absent-minded kisses when the occasion demanded. He entranced us with his story of running away from home when he was young to join the circus. He achieved billing as "Ellsworth, the Boy Wonder" for balancing chairs and tables on his chin. I never witnessed him doing it (he said he was out of practice), so we had to be satisfied with the broomstick on his nose, which he was able to hold there for over a minute.

After he left the circus, he performed as a singer and did recitations and skits. During that time he entertained on a Mississippi riverboat, and was later beckoned by Hollywood agents, as were many actors of his time, to spend a warm winter in Southern California trying out for the motion pictures.

He was a great practical joker, one of which I remember well. He had a friend from Chautauqua by the name of Edmund Vance Cooke who had published a book of verse. Grandpa Plum gave me an autographed copy of the book one Christmas, then Mr. Cooke came to Birmingham, Michigan for a visit. I was elated by such proximity to the world of letters. Gramp took him on a tour of his "estate," and showed him a rare and exotic plant—a banana tree . . . in a Michigan back yard! (Gramp had purchased a large bunch of bananas, then tied them, one by one, to the branches of our old peach tree.)

As I grew up, he began to pay more attention to me. My theatrical ambitions and activities interested and amused him. In one of our conversations he stressed education. He advised me to give that high priority. Cutting short his schooling had been the worst mistake he ever made. It undermined his confidence. He could never be sure, while performing, he wouldn't make an ignorant error at a crucial moment. He also discouraged me from considering a theatrical career. As successful as he had been, it was more often frustrating and heartbreaking.

Chautauqua, like vaudeville, faded out as the movies took over and established the entertainment industry. The first Edison film had been shown in 1896 in New York, and within one generation movies had become the entertainment of choice. Jobs became fewer and fewer. In the summer of 1926 when I was twelve, my Uncle Don, Aunt Mary, Uncle Phil, Gramma and I took a trip to Dunkirk, Ohio, in Don's old Packard to see Gramp in Chautauqua. To me it seemed like a journey to the other side of Nowhere, but actually it appears on the map to be about 100 miles from Birmingham. Dunkirk, a charming little Midwestern town, had a white clap-board hotel where all the actors stayed.

It was a warm summer night, and the show tent was full of lights, music and many friendly, excited townspeople. How proud I was to be related to one of the stars! His act included singing, recitations, and a comedy skit with a pretty lady who played the big sister to his bratty little boy. I remember the audience loved it.

Alas, the Chautauqua died! Thereafter, Grampa Plum occasionally did shows for local groups. I remember his famous monologue, "The Falling Star" during one such evening, and it brought tears to the eyes of his audience.

"Elegant" was a word I will always associate with him. Where many would say "fine," Grandpa Plum would say "elegant." In his red smoking jacket with the velvet lapels, holding his cigar in his slim veined hands, he *was* elegant. This is how I remember him—his aristocratic eccentricities, his countless jokes, his absent-minded foibles that we all laughed at and loved. He was a true prototype of many of the flamboyant Hollywood stars we know and love today.

REED CALLISTER

TAD CALLISTER

26 A Tower of Generosity
by Tad R. Callister

She pried the lid off the bucket of Kentucky Fried Chicken, and there was a $20 dollar bill draped over an extra-crispy drumstick. The elderly recipient of the meal said that my father faked amazement, and then blamed it on the absent-minded clerk at Colonel Sanders. Stories like hers, typical of thousands of others through the years, have been repeated frequently along with humble thanks.

Attorney Reed Callister had a custom of quietly dispensing kindness with an equally generous portion of a pixie-like humor. His financial help and habit of frequently taking meals to those in need became legend. In a world where lawyers often wear a mantle of cold-heartedness and arrogance, his example might be considered unique.

My dad passed on a simple philosophy. He said to us, "If you make an enemy, you make a mistake."

Born in 1901, he was one of the founding partners of KIEV Radio in Glendale, CA. When he was only 29 years old and a law student at George Washington University Law School in Washington, D.C., he was asked to appear before the Federal Communications Commission on behalf of Victor Dalton, a client of his brother-in-law David Cannon. Dalton had purchased two existing radio stations in Southern California, and had begun broadcasting from both without FCC permission.

Reed Callister was successful in obtaining a permit for the station in Inglewood but was disappointed to discover the ruling allowed only one permit per applicant. So the permit for the Glendale station was denied.

But my dad had been named after Utah's Senator Reed Smoot, a friend of the Callister family. So he decided to re-submit the application under his own name after contacting his old friend.

Senator Smoot reminded Commissioner Harold LaFount of the 5th Zone of the FCC, with jurisdiction over the western states, that his brother Ned had been instrumental in obtaining LaFount's appointment to the FCC as a commissioner several years earlier. So Dad's second application was swiftly approved.

When my dad completed law school, Dalton rewarded him by giving him and David Cannon the existing transmitter in Glendale. He told him that KNX Radio, a CBS network affiliate, owned an old set of five-story-tall steel broadcasting towers by their facilities on Hollywood Boulevard. They were needed for radio transmission, and that they were for sale.

So he offered KNX $250 dollars and they accepted. Then came the chore of relocating the towers some 30 miles away. My dad remembered paying a local blacksmith $35 dollars to have them dismantled, to relocate them, and then to re-erect them behind the Glendale Hotel off of Brand Boulevard in Glendale.

Prior to the move and installation, he made arrangements with the Glendale Hotel management for free rent in exchange for free advertisement. Then he rolled up his sleeves, working side-by-side with the blacksmith, both tackling the nearly impossible job of erecting these two huge towers. Dad personally poured all the cement.

Reed Callister, formerly a resident of Utah, had moved to Glendale after law school in order to work with his brother-in-law David Cannon, who became his law partner and co-owner of the radio station.

Their first time on the air was in the spring of 1931, and it began with the theme song, "The Daring Young Man On the Flying Trapeze." The program asked for musical requests to be called in from the radio audience, and that first broadcast proved several things—there were a lot of people listening, and everybody loved the idea.

That first program proved to be so popular the telephone lines jammed. They were tied up so completely, a complaint was filed by the telephone company with the FCC.

They answered the complaint by saying it obviously proved their broadcasts provided a community service.

The offices and broadcasting studios occupied the basement of the Glendale Hotel for the next 30 years. Then they constructed stairs leading to the first floor and moved upstairs.

The long list of on-the-air personalities who began their years in broadcasting on the KIEV staff reads like the "Who's Who in Southern California Radio History." Many may still remember Dick Whittinghill, later of KMPC; Jack Narz, who became a national television game show host; Don Rickles of NBC comedy fame; Dick Sinclair, for many years the voice of KFI Radio and KTLA television, who then returned after a 26-year absence to become KIEV's program director; Paul Wallach; and the venerable George Putnam.

A broadcasting giant in the making even before he finished law school, a highly revered attorney, a church leader and a day-to-day philanthropist, my father Reed Callister left an unforgettable imprint from the elderly lady down the street, to municipal judges, to broadcasting moguls across the country.

No matter who they were, his towering generosity touched them all.

GLENN ACKERMAN

27 Invisibility and Fame
by Glenn Ackerman

There is probably no one who has not fantasized about what it would feel like to be invisible. I think I have an idea, since it was a part of my challenge as an undercover vice detective, assigned to the Los Angeles Police Department's Administrative Vice Division. My responsibility was to penetrate and bring down several large-scale call girl organizations. It proved to be no easy task.

These are highly lucrative operations, and the pimps and madams who run them take every precaution to ensure they're not compromised by law enforcement efforts.

The only way I could succeed was by being a "pod" person, a resourceful and highly flexible chameleon. I created and acted out different convincing and airtight personas, otherwise known as "covers" in police vernacular.

One of my most effective covers was that of Lester Bernstein, M.D., who also happened to be, in *my* incarnation, a high line call girl trick and "steerer." A steerer is someone who directs business to a madam or pimp in return for free "action" or a cut of the fee. Professionals of all stripes (including clergymen) are call girl clients, and physicians are no exception. As I played Dr. Bernstein, he was simply a very active steerer who was well-known in the business. I was originally "duked in" to the "life" by a well-known madam we had put the squeeze on.

Dr. Bernstein came to life when I made an arrangement with a physician I knew who agreed to take me on as his "partner." Then I assumed the State of Board of Medical Examiners license number of the real Dr. Lester Bernstein, who had moved to Hawaii many years before and subsequently died there.

Dr. Bernstein was originally from San Diego, and had been in Hawaii many years prior to his death. There was virtually zero chance that any of the players knew the original Bernstein. So with the cooperation of the Department of Motor Vehicles, I received my fake driver's license in his name, and the L.A.P.D.'s Scientific Investigation Division created all of the bogus documents I would need to render my new identity completely airtight.

When anyone called my friend's medical office and asked to speak to Dr. Bernstein, they were told he was in surgery, making rounds, or with a patient. They promised he would call back as soon as he was free.

I had my cover. The rest was up to me.

Using that and other covers, I cut an ever-widening swath through the organized prostitution scene in Los Angeles for several years, even to bringing down one of the most infamous—Madam Alex.

I was the first one to arrest Madam Alex on a felony (pimping and pandering) in 1972. Her real name was Elizabeth Adams, and at that time she was beginning to make a name for herself as a high line madam. After I left Administative Vice in 1973, Alex stayed in the business off and on by becoming an informant for Administrative Vice cops.

Heidi Fleiss got her start as a call girl working for Alex, who by that time had solidified her reputation as the biggest madam in Los Angeles. When Heidi came to my attention she was bragging in the Los Angeles Times that she had supplanted Alex as *THE* "Madam to the Stars."

As Dr. Bernstein, I could walk into rooms filled with "players," people in the life of prostitution, without them raising an eyebrow. Visualize, if you will, a school of fish twisting and turning in unison from deep in the shadows of a murky pool, when a fish just like them joins the school and instantly becomes a part of their complex choreography. The other fish see only something that looks and moves like them, and so they take no notice. Sometimes that other fish is a shark in disguise. In a like manner, as a member of the police department, I had to become...invisible.

It was one of the most exhilarating experiences I have ever had. But it was not to last. Fame or near fame is fleeting. Unfortunately, so is obscurity or invisibility. In the 20 years since that time, I climbed the ranks to senior captain, and then became the commanding officer of the Administration Vice Division. I had come full circle.

There are 18 small geographic vice units, one in each area or precinct, that handle streetwalkers of all kinds. Ad Vice, as it is known, is the "Big Leagues." It has citywide jurisdiction, is responsible for both vice intelligence and enforcement, and focuses on major organized vice, whether it be prostitution, or gambling, or the like.

Just to be in Ad Vice means you have arrived, and its commanding officer ranks at the head of the pack in terms of prestige.

When I came back to Ad Vice there were few if any prostitution investigations going on. They hadn't been a priority of the previous C.O., which is why Heidi had been operating with impunity. When she gave that interview to the *Times*, I changed that focus in a heartbeat. I called the Prostitution Section together and told them they would take Heidi down, and if they couldn't figure out how to do it, I would.

Heidi had some low-level Mafia connections and was also believed to be laundering huge amounts of money through her pediatrician father. The investigation eventually involved a task force that included the L.A.P.D.'s Organized Crime Intelligence Division, and the IRS, as well as Ad Vice. It was then that television and the newspapers staged one of the most intense media frenzies the nation has ever witnessed.

As commander, with the kind of experiences I'd had, I became the departmental spokesman in relation to the Fleiss investigation, as well as running the investigation and the department. During those months of 1993, I held countless press conferences and gave over a hundred televised interviews on every show from *Hard Copy* to those from the British Broadcasting Corporation. I debated with feminist attorney Gloria Allred on the *Larry King Live* program, and appeared on the *Good Day L.A.* show in relation to the issue of discriminatory enforcement.

The resulting "fame" caused me a total loss of privacy, and for many months people would approach me in the mall or the supermarket, the gas station, or right on the sidewalk with comments like, "You're the cop I saw on TV," or "You're the D.A. in the Heidi Fleiss case. Why are you hassling those poor girls?" It became one of the most unnerving experiences of my life, the precise opposite of my previous and wonderful invisibility. It was something akin to appearing naked in public.

Fame has been called "The Bitch Goddess." In my experience, you can drop the "Goddess" part. As someone who was almost famous for a bit more than 15 minutes, I can't fathom why so many yearn for a condition that extracts such a heavy toll and gives virtually *nothing* in return.

For me, my most exhilarating memories will always be those when I played the invisible man.

ASTRONAUT RICK SEARFOSS

Astronaut Rick Searfoss, Colonel, USAF Retired, piloted two Space Shuttle missions. He also commanded a third flight, the STS-90 "Neurolab" mission on Columbia. Now a professional speaker, consultant, and space entrepreneur, he focuses on leadership, teamwork, and personal excellence. Contact him at Mach 25 Leadership, 661-821-0301, email: searfoss5@earthlink.net, or web site: www.astronautspeaker.com.

28 From Cold Warrior Opponents to Space Explorer Colleagues
by Astronaut Rick Searfoss

"Range two feet, rate point one foot per second, timing good, lineup good." Twenty seconds later, "contact, soft dock." We're there. Gazing out of Space Shuttle Atlantis' overhead windows I see a breathtaking sight, the Russian space station Mir. We've just docked with her as together we hurtle around planet Earth 240 miles up at 17,500 miles per hour.

As pilot on mission STS-76, I'm helping deliver American scientist-astronaut Shannon Lucid to begin a six-month stay in space. Fleeting thoughts come to me of how unbelievable it all seems. Not just that we've safely completed the orbital join-up of two quarter million pound behemoths, Atlantis and the Mir. It's more amazing that we're even doing this at all, less than ten years after I as a U.S. Air Force fighter pilot lined up across the Iron Curtain from the cosmonaut commander of Mir, himself a former Soviet fighter pilot.

Growing up in the sixties I remember from an early age the ever-present Cold War, the threat posed by the Soviet Union, and our mutual fear and distrust. Living on a Strategic Air Command base as the son of an Air Force pilot, I was even more aware of those realities than most kids. Space and the dramatic race to put humans on the moon also enthralled me. This awareness and interest blossomed into a desire to become an Air Force pilot and also to fly in space as an astronaut.

During the eighties when I was a mission-ready F-111 "Aardvark" attack fighter pilot stationed in England, the Cold War still hung over our heads. We knew that at any time it could turn hot. Our training was intense, serious, and focused. During my three years in England our base lost four crewmembers killed in training. We faced a foe with far larger numbers of troops and weapons. The Russians were the enemy, they had always been the enemy during my entire lifetime, and it didn't look like the situation would change anytime soon.

But almost overnight things did change for the better as Cold War tensions eased, the Iron Curtain fell, and the old Soviet Union broke apart. By then I had finished the year-long Test Pilot School and was anxiously awaiting news from NASA whether I had been accepted into the 1990 astronaut class. The word came. Yes! I was going to Houston to become an astronaut! It was a big transition, from military attack and test missions to piloting NASA spacecraft.

About the same time, a gentleman named Yuri Onufrienko was also making a transition. As a Su-17 "Fitter" ground attack pilot, he had a military background similar to mine. The F-111 and Su-17 had almost the exact same mission: attack enemy targets from the air after ingressing at low altitude and high speed. Rightfully proud of the great accomplishments of the Soviet space program—first man

Launch of Atlantis on mission STS-76

in space, first spacewalk, many long duration missions—he too dreamed of flying in space. One day he received the exciting call that he would be moving to the Yuri Gagarin Training Center in Star City outside Moscow to become a cosmonaut.

After I'd completed my first space flight on Columbia in 1993, we began to hear very interesting rumors of plans to work together with the Russians. Still with Cold War holdover attitudes, I couldn't quite see us really working together effectively. And in fact, it was a slow, sometimes fitful start as each side tried to scope out the other's motivations. Slowly the trust and relationships built. First we exchanged crewmembers—a U.S. astronaut launching on a Soyuz and a Russian cosmonaut joining a Shuttle mission. Then a rendezvous, but no docking. Later the first docking of the Shuttle to Mir. Finally, my second mission in the spring of 1996, a docking, five days linked together transferring supplies, a spacewalk from the Shuttle to the Mir, and dropping off Shannon for a long duration stay aboard Mir.

July 1995, on a sticky, hot Houston Saturday afternoon, with everyone standing around the grill chatting, we drip due to the legendary Texas Gulf Coast humidity. Some of us, living in much cooler climes, feel it more than others. Amidst the normal banter and the occasional Texas "howdy," you can hear some heavily accented, slowly spoken English or halting, American-accented Russian. It's the first get-together, the chance to meet the Russian cosmonauts who will be aboard Mir when we take Atlantis up to dock. Commander Yuri Onufrienko, his flight engineer Yuri Usachev, and their two backup crewmembers have just arrived in Houston for a ten-day training trip. They'll learn the basics of Space Shuttle systems and the joint procedures we'll perform together. To kick it off our crew hosts a traditional Texas barbecue. Tentatively at first, we get to know one another. The big dose of down-home hospitality helps break the ice, and by the end of the day I'm thinking that these guys are all right, this ought to work out just fine. They're certainly far from the ogres we'd been conditioned to believe they were when as kids we had to dive under our desks during Cold War civil defense drills!

A few months later, and the six of us on the STS-76 crew have just finished the long flight from Houston to Moscow. It's early on a chilly, drizzly Russian October morning, far different from the Houston heat. Moscow is gray and nondescript. Right across the street from the hotel there's an outdoor museum of Russian military equipment. I'd seen plenty of intelligence photographs, but to look out my hotel window at the exact type of surface-to-air missiles these guys built to blow away my old squadron buddies and me strikes me as surreal and more than a little dreary on that cold, gray day.

But the next morning dawns brilliantly clear and crisp, a perfect fall day just like the ones I used to enjoy in New Hampshire as a child. As we drive out into the birch-covered countryside on the way to Star City, I begin to appreciate the natural beauty of this northern land, not really so different from the northern state in which I grew up. After a couple hours drive we arrive at a guard shack manned by olive drab and red trim cloaked soldiers. A short pause to reflect and think—this spot used to be one of the most secret and closely guarded installations in the entire Soviet Union! But we're waved through quickly and soon meet with the two Yuris and the staff who will conduct our training. Just like the cosmonauts received a basic orientation on the Space Shuttle, we'll learn about the Mir and its systems.

At one point Yuri Onufrienko, Kevin Chilton, who was the STS-76 commander, Yuri's backup Vasily Tsibliyev, and I compare notes on our flying experiences. All four of us were fighter pilots who had been stationed at spots right across the fence from the other, even seeing the other country's aircraft from time to time over the Baltic Sea. Three of us were "swing-wingers," or pilots of variable-geometry, very high-speed aircraft. Kevin, as an F-15 pilot the only exception, takes some grief as I gamely try to translate into Russian for my swing-wing colleagues an old F-111 saying, "If your wings don't swing, you ain't squat." Then Vasily offers some serious thoughts as he relates how grateful he is that our political leaders had not unleashed our military forces against each other. A time both for sober reflection as we ponder unpleasant alternatives and thankful agreement that things worked out as they did.

No barbecues, but still plenty of hospitality, Russian style. I really developed a liking for borscht! Finally, the big going-away party the night before we were to leave, with a wonderful smorgasbord and, this being Russia, much vodka. One of our hosts, noticing Shannon and me toasting with orange juice, both of us for personal religious reasons, politely and curiously asks why. As we explain, he nods his understanding. I go out on a limb to ask him if he has a religion or believes in God. Remember, this person would have in the past been a prime example of the best the old Soviet system had to offer, the perfect "new Soviet man," officially denying any sort of faith in a Supreme Being. After a reflective pause, the thoughtful response comes, "I do not have a religion. We have not been taught these things. But I do believe there is a God." His sincere and reverent response touches me to the depths of my soul.

Six months later, following a successful docking, we joyously open the hatch to once again greet our brethren, this time not in Houston, not in Star City, but in the sublimely beautiful environment of space. Floating effortlessly between our two spacecraft, carrying each other's flags, Shannon's equipment, and supplies for Mir, we all work together diligently fourteen hours a day to accomplish every mission objective. In space we again treat one another with our own brands of hospitality. Dinner on board Atlantis—dehydrated shrimp cocktail, freeze-dried asparagus, and thermal-stabilized steak. Dinner on board Mir—a hearty stew, delicious warm Russian bread, and a delightfully sweet berry dessert from a squeeze tube.

With the time together in space passing all too quickly, before long five American astronauts must depart with Atlantis, leaving Shannon to stay six months aboard Mir, breaking both the U.S. overall and worldwide women's human space endurance records. For me the most memorable aspect of the whole adventure, particularly given my prior military experience, is that I've been privileged to participate in such an incredibly historic episode—the U.S. and Russia working together cooperatively in space. The change from cold warrior opponents to space explorer colleagues is now complete.

One could say that forty-five years of Cold War anxiety and concerns, certainly not a delectable state of affairs, represented a "chopped liver" relationship between America and the Soviet Union. And many of us, I believe, felt then that the bill of fare might never change. Yet in a very short period of time, changing conditions led to an improved menu. Russia still faces daunting challenges. And America, like the rest of the world, still faces many uncertainties and worries. Most often though, our darkest fears do not come to pass, but situations resolve themselves better than we would've anticipated. While it may not yet be filet mignon every night in this particular international relationship, the entree is far more palatable now than it used to be! This cold warrior, for one, is very thankful.

DR. HARRIS DONE

29 Ambassadors of Good Teeth
by Harris Done, D.D.S.

With tears in her eyes, the woman approached me and placed a package of rare Guatemalan chocolates in my hands, telling me in Spanish that this was her gift of appreciation and love for what we were doing. The students from the USC School of Dentistry were very moved, considering how much it must have cost her. It represented about a year's worth of her meager earnings. Our sacrifice to be there was nothing compared to what she had just done. She still couldn't believe anyone would come halfway around the world and donate their time to fix her children's teeth.

Since we founded this worldwide effort at USC over a generation ago, it has become my hobby. I must be a boring person with very few interests in life, but to me this is fun.

In 1967, one of the country's great religious leaders proposed an idea whereby everybody would benefit. Spencer W. Kimball laid out a plan for doctors and dentists to travel to the Indians of the Southwest and to countries south of the border and voluntarily serve those in great need of health-care assistance.

The appreciation for this effort has been reflected many fold by the local citizens, the professionals of the area in need of technical updating, by the United States Government in its attempt to reach out diplomatically to these people, by the dental professionals, and by the students themselves. Those involved see a large number of patients in a very short time, and in the process, develop a strong sense of caring. The program really changes the lives of the students who get involved. They become truly community-minded and make many wonderful, international friends, both for themselves and for our country.

The assistance offered by seasoned dentists, senior dental students and the faculty members from the University of Southern California is under the auspices of Ayuda, which means "help" in Spanish. Ayuda, Inc. has organized at least one excursion per year since its beginning to destinations such as Mexico, Belize, Honduras, Guatemala and has even extended its influence to China. It began as a service to the native population of Arizona, and then extended to Guatemala, but its purpose has since been expanded, both medical and dental, to needy people throughout North and South America.

One such trip in 1999 was to Belize in Central America, formerly British Honduras, a trip that covered over 3,500 miles. A group of 17 students under my supervision spend two weeks working on the children of that area. It is partly funded by volunteers who pay their own plane fare, by Rotary International, and by donations from individuals amounting to over $10,000. The students selected received "scholarship" money of $600 each which paid for local transportation, hotels and meals, allowing them to afford to go on their spring break. It cost each dental student $430 for the round trip air fare, plus about two hundred for incidental expenses. No government funds were involved, and the students took their own equipment.

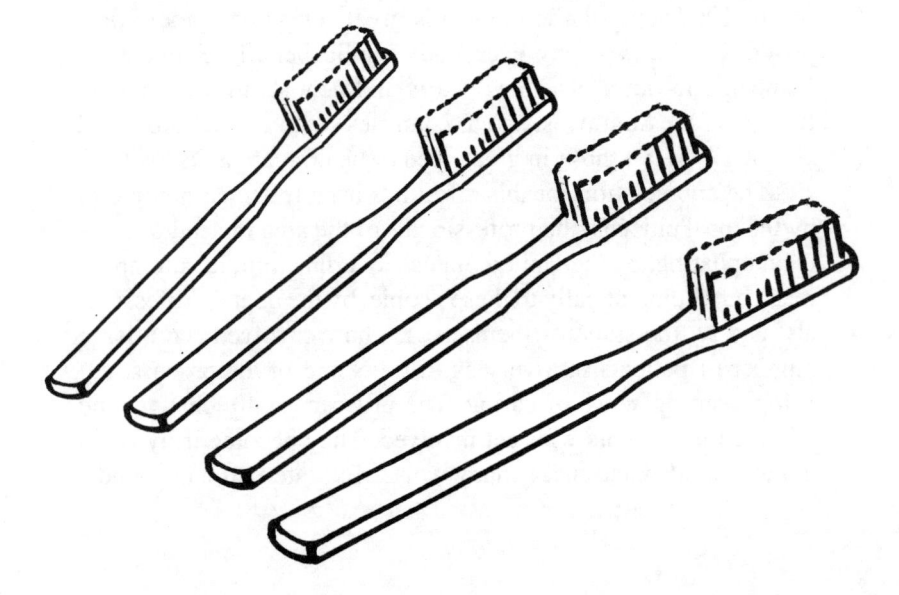

We took 1,500 donated toothbrushes with us, and the team distributed about 300 of them to each school we visited. Altogether there were 907 patients treated during their stay that year, and it has been estimated that one-tenth of Belize's population has received treatement since the inception of Ayuda. Each time these countries are visited, we leave behind clinical instruction and facilities to continue the work year-round.

Ayuda extends to our local needy children as well. Over 30,000 young students in Orange County, California, between 5 and 12 years of age go one Saturday a month and line up for treatment in one of the 12 to 20 clinics set up around the county.

In August of 2000, we took American dentisty behind the Bamboo Curtain. For 10 days we played dental Marco Polos and visited two major universities in an area covered by 20 government hospitals and the Sun Yat-sen Dental School. We were able to lay the groundwork for a humanitarian outreach between the faculty and students of USC and their counterparts in China. The next August a group of 12 students visited for 17 days, attended lectures, organized a tour, and with their new Chinese friends, gave treatment to the poor in outlying areas.

It all came about due to one of my patients from Canton who had obtained an invitation from the Chinese government for him to act as a consultant to modernize dental operations in government hospitals. With that I was able to arrange the tour with Ayuda and Rotary International sponsorship. Currently, China represents about 21 percent of the world's population. Prior to our leaving, we had the privilege of being visited by Dr. Ling Je Qi, dean of the Sun Yat-sen Dental School, on the USC campus.

I have seldom seen a program with such a powerful potential for good throughout the world, benefiting so many people, that upgrades so many lives, and in which there is so much joy and good feeling.

PATTY and ERNIE WECKBAUGH

30 Woman's Place Is In the House ...or the Senate!

by Ernie & Patty Weckbaugh

"I figured I could fight them better if I joined them. So here I am." Lynn Woolsey, Representative from the 6th Congressional District in northern California, is the first former welfare mother to be elected to Congress. Twenty-five years before, after her divorce, she was forced to go on welfare for three years to support herself and her three small children.

In 1962, she had left the University of Washington before graduating to help the man she married get through college. The couple then moved to San Francisco where her husband became a successful stockbroker. Meanwhile, she stayed at home in affluent Marin County and gave birth to three children in five years. Their lifestyle put them within easy reach of the American Dream.

But her husband began suffering from psychological problems. Depression, and the accompanying anxiety and insecurity cost him his job and destroyed their marriage. Unable to support his family, he simply abandoned them, and her sweet dream turned into a tragic nightmare.

She was forced to sell their four-bedroom home to pay her bills, which left her with only $300, a washer and a dryer. She had to take a low-paying secretarial job and turn to welfare and food stamps to supplement her income. It was this experience, with its myriad of associated problems, that politicized her.

"I became somewhat left of center about that time," she said. "I began to believe government was supposed to be in business to help people who needed assistance."

Woolsey remarried in 1971 and moved to Petaluma, California. She earned a business degree from the University of San Francisco and started her own employment agency in 1980. She ran for the Petaluma City Council in 1984 and won that election—and the next one, too. *That* election, as Neil Armstrong said as he stepped onto the surface of the moon, was a giant leap.

In 1992 she decided to run for the Congressional seat vacated by Barbara Boxer who had just won the election to the United States Senate. Woolsey ran on the platform that called for programs to train people for jobs that pay a "living wage." She won with a powerful 67 percent majority.

Shortly after her arrival in Washington, D.C., she was among the handful of Congresswomen who demanded that the previously all-male Capitol Hill gymnasium offer facilities for women. Shortly thereafter, she became the first woman to play on the congressional basketball team, although her performance didn't match her skills as a legislator. Her memory of it was, "I didn't score any points, but at least I didn't foul anyone."

Although first-year Representatives seldom write laws, she proposed a measure right away that cracked down on "deadbeat dads."

"Now, if you don't make child-support payments," she insisted, "it will go against your credit record." Compelled by her personal experiences as a welfare mother, Rep. Woolsey later introduced her own comprehensive welfare bill titled: "Working Off Welfare Act of 1994."

Within the seven months following the 1992 election, she became one of only five freshmen on the special House-Senate Conference Committee that painfully pounded out the federal budget. She had developed more clout than some members with many more years of seniority. Always concerned about how the acts of Congress will affect people, she was able, as a committee member, to help protect those very same, frequently endangered social programs that had saved her and her children so many years before.

For all of her vigorous and effective activity, she was honored by a coalition of national education groups with the "Outstanding New Member (of Congress) Award." for 1993.

"I have 'walked the walk' in the area of reform in the welfare system," she says. "It was for this reason I decided to run for election to Congress in the first place."

PATTY WECKBAUGH

31 It's *Her* Business
by Patty Weckbaugh

One of my best friends in college had the opportunity to establish a business after she married and moved to Dallas, Texas. It was a giftware business that required her to travel frequently to Western Europe to deal with silver and porcelain craftsmen and manufacturers.

France is famous for its prized porcelain, and also as the land of the chauvinists. Being a woman, and an American, she knew she already had two strikes against her. Nicholas Chauvin became famous for his fanatic loyalty to Napoleon I, even long after his hero was exiled in disgrace. His name became synonymous with fierce loyalty to lost causes, such as the myth of male superiority.

Sandy's business was called the Silver Leopard, where she displayed all forms of imported, decorative silver and porcelain houseware, specializing in hand-painted porcelain boxes. They come from Limoges, a small French town whose craftsmen create this exquisite giftware in ateliers throughout the countryside.

Her first trip there was in the mid-1980s, and she took another woman with her, which proved to be frustrating. Everyone she needed to do business with was a man, who considered them just a couple of American housewives trying to shop for bargains.

So on the next trip she took her husband. He was the only person anyone wanted to deal with. He kept repeating to the Frenchmen, over and over, "It's *her* business. Talk to *her*." After several trips they finally got the idea, although a business *woman* still remains an amusing novelty to them.

Sandy's background was in theatre arts, and she dreamed of

one day becoming a professional stage or film director. But when she graduated from college in 1960 there were few female directors, and she decided perhaps it was an "impossible dream." Although she had no business classes in college, she put business people on her staff when she started her venture into gift retailing and she learned from them. Her Dallas store was soon grossing over two-million a year.

Always involved in community little theatre productions and community affairs over the years, she was asked to chair the Dallas Cotton Bowl Parade Committee. Whenever she had watched the parade on television, as a native Californian she compared it, not too favorably, with Pasadena's Rose Parade. Since the major TV Networks were going to be in Dallas to cover the parade before the nationally televised Cotton Bowl game, Sandy had confidence that she could make major improvements.

But the reaction to a woman taking over was quite predictable. The Cotton Bowl Football Committee with whom she met was composed of ex-football players from different universities in Texas. They had only dealt in previous years with other ex-athletes. They promptly dismissed her with the attitude of, "Why don't you just go away and 'do your little parade' and don't bother us." Once again Sandy discovered that chauvinism was not dead.

But improve it she did, and successfully presided over the last two years of the parade before it was cancelled.

Though not a feminist, Sandy was used to overcoming these kinds of barriers and disappointments. When they were married, her husband ran a large Dallas-based contracting firm making important corporate installations worldwide. With Sandy's personable nature and marketable skills, she expressed her eagerness to be involved in *his* business. So she was given a job within the marketing and advertising staff.

But partnership problems soon saw their business finances begin to slowly dissolve away into the hands of lawyers. After several years of court trials, they saw all of their opportunites and assets disappear as if in a puff of smoke.

It was then that the idea of the retail business began to develop in Sandy's mind, after she had done a considerable amount of market research. She determined that several of the local businesses were eager to support and cooperate with her intended enterprise after she showed them how it would benefit them. Many of them were willing to have a display case of her exquisite merchandise installed in the lobby of their establishments if she would share 50 percent of the retail price with them. The exposure to such a large number of established local customers rapidly spread the Silver Leopard name and the quality of their giftware, and she was successful almost from the start.

It was then the traditional roles in business started to reverse. Her ex-president/CEO husband began to serve as the credibility factor during those first trips to France. Thanks to their strong marriage relationship and his considerable business acumen, they decided to integrate his skills into her business development and planning needs. Over the next few years her husband became her junior partner and business manager.

Everybody, however, knew for a fact . . . "it's *her* business."

RAY SCHNIEDERS

32 No Mountain Too High
by Ray Schnieders

I have a little different feeling about retirement, I guess, than most people do. When I left the Fire Department at age 55, I figured it was time for me to completely change my lifestyle. This was my chance to see the world.

I have always enjoyed climbing. I've climbed my share of ladders in my time, but it's really mountains that have always appealed to me, mountains like Mount Kilimanjaro in Africa, 19,340 feet high, which I climbed in 1989.

I usually travel solo, but I was accompanied that time by two people from Germany and two from Norway on the final part of my ascent to the top. I don't have much trouble with high altitudes. It doesn't make me ill as it does some people, just the normal difficulty in breathing. But I wasn't prepared for the extreme cold. It was minus 30 degrees counting the wind chill.

Climbing above 18,000 feet can be a serious health hazard. It forces you to work with less than half of your normal oxygen supply. You experience shortness of breath, nausea, insomnia and headaches. Frostbite becomes more of a problem because less oxygen means your body generates less heat.

You have to be careful with your coordination and judgment. Accidents and falls that normally wouldn't happen occur quite often at very high altitudes. Generally, the more time you spend above 20,000 feet, the worse you feel. Your body never fully adjusts to that environment.

Strange things can happen to you in the rarified air, and the older person often enjoys an advantage over the robust 20-year old. The older climber knows how to perform when feeling less than 100 percent. I can pace myself more naturally, exerting only the energy necessary, and I never compete to be the first one up the hill.

The constant feeling of being ill isn't something new to older climbers. Their age and experience usually pays off. Nonetheless, trying to predict your performance at high altitude can only be a guess. The five-day trek to the top of Kilimanjaro involved walking about 45 to 50 miles. Anyone who is reasonably fit should be able to do it. All that's needed is a lot of determination.

Our group walked from the hotel to the Managu Gate, which is the beginning point of the ascent at 6,000 feet. With guides and porters, we entered the Kilimanjaro National Park and hiked through the rain forest.

The unique vegetation, including orchids growing wild in the forest, and the spectacular scenery made the trek unforgettable. We spent the first night at Mandara Hut, which is at about 9,000 feet.

The next day the group left the rain forest early in the morning. We slowly climbed above the treeline onto the tundra (permanently frozen ground). Mount Kilimanjaro is only three degrees above the equator, yet its peak is permanently covered with ice and snow.

It took us about five hours to walk the seven miles to Horombo Hut at 12,340 feet. The altitude began to affect us there, so we rested a lot. Another early start on the third day put us on the volcanic ash of the "saddle," which has the appearance of a desert.

The weather over this stretch can really change, dropping to extreme cold quite rapidly. But we took plenty of warm clothing for the last night's stay in the hut, just below Kibo, at 15,520 feet. The final part of our ascent began at 1 a.m. the next morning.

We went to Gilman's Point and from there to the summit, Uruhu, at 19,340 feet. This was the most tiring part of the climb. It took us over five hours to reach Gilman, the first peak. In another hour we reached Uruhu, the highest point on the continent of Africa. The sunrise, slowly illuminating the snow and ice scenery, was breathtaking.

We rested for the night before we descended to Horombo Hut. The rest of the downward trek took only one day, putting everyone back in the hotel by late afternoon. The long, hot bath and a relaxing evening never felt so good. The only bad news was a bit of frostbite on my face, which caused it to peel like sunburn.

During the rest of the trip we encountered a variety of animals, including elephants, which seldom bother anyone. One passed through our camp one night and stepped on the edge of my tent. Fortunately, nothing was damaged. The monkeys were all around us, stealing everything they could carry.

What makes all this possible is that I act as my own travel agent. The trip to Africa might have cost as much as $9,000 through an agent. But by contracting the airfare myself, and piecing it together once I got there, I did it all for less than $2,000.

To see the world from the top of its mountains, you can start with a low budget and wind up with a high adventure.

In La Canada-Flintridge, California, Jon Inskeep is a neighbor of mine, and is also a mountain climbing and rescue enthusiast.

Jon Inskeep can tell you that life isn't all applause and gratitude for mountain rescuers.

He learned the hard way once as he rappelled from the top of a cliff to reach a "cliffhanger," a person who tries to climb a rock wall and becomes too frightened halfway up to move.

"It was a hot summer day, and I was packing about 50 pounds of gear," he said. "All of it was necessary to secure and lift the young boy below me, who was clinging desperately to the face of the cliff.

"As I reached him, struggling to position myself over him with a safety rope, he looked up angrily and shouted, 'Watch it, man, you're dripping sweat on me!'"

Inskeep began mountain climbing as a form of recreation his family could share.

"We lived in Lancaster, California, in the high desert," he said. "We found so many interesting peaks available to us in the nearby area that climbing became almost a regular weekend family activity."

After moving to La Canada in 1968, Inskeep joined the Sierra Madre Search and Rescue Team in 1972.

"It used to be that we thought 10-year members were the old-timers. Now many of us have been there much longer than that."

Today, Inskeep is involved in the formation of a new climbing organization, The California Mountaineering Club. He has been at the Jet Propulsion Laboratory as an engineer since moving to La Canada, a specialist in instrumentation systems. He spent the eight years before that in JPL's test facility at Edwards Air Force Base in the Lancaster/Palmdale area.

He refers to himself as a "peak bagger" who challenges himself to go to the top of as many of the world's mountains as possible. His first major climb was in 1978 to the summit of Mt. McKinley in Alaska, 20,300 feet, a month-long expedition. In untypically clear weather—McKinley's summit is almost always covered with clouds—Inskeep and his climbing companions were able to record the event on film. Nevertheless, he almost lost a toe to frostbite from the experience.

His climbing party flew there in a skiplane from Talkeetna and landed on the nearby glacier. "We were never off the ice and snow, nor did we see anything green or brown for the next three weeks," he remembered.

Most recently, he climbed Mt. Kilimanjaro, like I did in 1989. Inskeep went with his oldest son Mike. "Although the mountain rises to more than 19,000 feet, it's more of a hike than a climb," he said. He climbed to the top of all the high points in each state west of the Rockies, except Idaho. "There are no *real* mountains east of the Rockies. I've climbed about 100 peaks in the Sierra, including 14 on the West Coast that exceed 14,000 feet. All but Washington's Mt. Rainier are in California.

"The east face of Mt. Whitney is its most spectacular side. It's sheer rock climbing all the way," he said. "Originally, we climbed Whitney's east face as a 'warm-up' for tackling Wyoming's Grand Teton in 1981."

After climbing several other Sierra peaks for practice, he found that the final ascent of "The Grand" wasn't nearly as challenging as the ones he had worked out on.

The year of a severe drought in Montana, Wyoming and Utah, Inskeep traveled there to climb the high points of those three states. "It was tough on the people who lived there, but it was the perfect condition for a mountaineer. There wasn't a cloud in the sky anywhere we climbed.

"We went to the big island of Hawaii, and while my wife was having her hair done one morning, I hiked to the top of its highest point, 13,796 foot Mauna Kea," he said. "You can drive a car to the 9,000 foot level. But my rental car was so underpowered, I had to go up backwards most of the way."

In 1983, Jon and his middle son Jon, Jr., reached the summits of the Matterhorn and Mont Blanc in Europe. Jon hasn't climbed with his dad since.

"We decided to attempt the Matterhorn without a guide," Jon, Sr. said, "because all of them were booked up for over a week. The weather had been so bad, they insisted each climber have his own guide, which is rather expensive. Jon and I went part way up to take a look and, suddenly, the weather cleared up. So we went for it.

"It was not an easy climb. The higher we went, the harder it got. But the closeness of the summit made us want to push on. The top was a narrow rock that dropped off vertically on all sides. We were very exposed," he said.

With their descent completed, father and son visited the Zermatt Climbers Museum where Jon, Jr. encountered numerous life stories and photos about every famous Swiss climber, recounting where and how they'd lost their lives. Most had died in mountaineering accidents, many of them on the Matterhorn.

"Slowly my son began to realize he had just covered the ground that had claimed the lives of most of these 'experts.' It was all I could do to talk him into staying for our other ascent up Mont Blanc," he said. "As luck would have it, that climb was worse than the Matterhorn. It was August, and all the easy-climbing snow that had filled the valleys had turned into treacherous ice walls, with open crevasses below.

"I had promised Jon we would climb this time only if we had a guide, but the guide we hired was an idiot and only made matters worse. So when Jon returned home, he gave away all his climbing gear and took up bicycle racing as a hobby."

On another climb up the east face of Mt. Whitney, Jon was climbing with a group of about six, including his son Mike. A daypack that was set on the edge of the trail during a rest break was accidently kicked over the ledge and bounced hundreds of feet out of sight down the mountainside. Jon realized to his dismay as he glanced around—it was *his* pack. It had all his warm clothing and food inside.

A few days later, after returning home and feeling very dejected, his doorbell rang. There on the porch stood a man holding the fallen pack. He expressed his sincere appreciation and said, "A group of us from church decided to hike up the mountainside last Saturday, only to find out too late that we really didn't know what we were doing." the man said. "We had climbed too far before we realized we hadn't taken enough food or extra clothing for protection against the cold wind.

"So we gathered in a circle on the trail," he said, "and knelt down in prayer. At the very moment we all said 'Amen,' the most miraculous thing happened. From out of the heavens came this package full of exactly what we had prayed for.

"When we opened it we shouted 'Hallelujah!',", he said, "and in unison we all praised God. And then, on further examination, we realized it belonged to you, since it contained your identification tag with this address. I hope you don't mind that we ate your food and wore your clothing. We took up a collection to pay for it. It's in an envelope inside.

" God bless you," he said to Jon, and left.

ERNIE WECKBAUGH

33 Against *All* Odds
by Ernie Weckbaugh

Hollywood actress Angel Harper, born in the Harlem section of New York City, is someone who has overcome all the odds and won. Being poor, black and female, she started with few advantages. But in sharp contrast to her mother's generation, she was able to graduate from Cornell University after attending on a full scholarship. She had attended a private Catholic high school, but had to work as a dietary assistant at a hospital to be able to pay the tuition.

She took no college-preparatory courses, convinced all along she would never go to college. But people at the hospital said she should think about a pre-med course in college and apply to an equal opportunity program for minority students. So, when she found out that Cornell University in Ithaca, New York, offered one called COSEP, she applied.

Realizing she was probably at the end of the waiting list, Harper decided to visit the Cornell campus. One of the students directed her to the head of the COSEP Program, who was very impressed with her interest in visiting the campus and made arrangements to put her up overnight.

She was so stunned by all the attention, she forgot to call her parents. When she didn't return home until the next day, she was in big trouble. But they quickly forgave her when they found out she had been accepted. "I was in shock. I had no idea how much that visit would help my chances," she said.

Unqualified, unprepared and without money, she bravely faced the challenge of heavy science courses and a lot of remedial work to make up for her lack of college-prep classes. She had been given a full scholarship as a pre-med student, which covered everything but meals and books, so she needed to continue working every summer to be able to afford it.

The turning point came when a friendly counselor made a remarkable suggestion when he found she was struggling in pre-med. He proposed that she take a double major, since she was receiving an "A" in every one of her communications classes. She knew she would lose her scholarship if she dropped pre-med, where her grades were poor.

Angel took the advice, continued to pull top grades in her communication courses and was able to keep her grade average high enough to graduate. The counselor assured her, "If you graduate, no one will care what you studied or how well you did. It's okay to do what you like to do. The fact that you were able to graduate from Cornell says *everything* about you."

His continual encouragement, plus knowing that no one thought she would be accepted to the school in the first place let alone graduate, kept her going and helped her get through.

Armed with her Bachelor of Science degree in communication (radio and television production), she moved to Washington, D.C. She successfully combined parallel careers in acting and business. Her communications background helped her land a job in sales and marketing. She received high recognition in corporate and feature films, commercial television and later as a writer. She authored a book titled *Master the Art of Cold Reading*.

In 1989 she moved again, this time to Los Angeles, where Hollywood welcomed her into the casts of such daytimes dramas as *The Young and the Restless, Generations* and *Santa Barbara*. Primetime opportunities followed with feature roles in *Anything But Love, Gabriel's Fire* and *FBI—The Untold Stories*. They discovered her talent as a stand-up comedienne at The Comedy Store and The Improv which rounded out her performance career.

In addition to entertaining young people with her cartoon voice-overs on *Batman, Ghostbusters, Captain Planet*, and a leading role in *Kevin's Kitchen* on *Nickelodeon*, she's taken time to reach out to others whose beginnings mirror hers. She has done public service announcements against child abuse, and was the producer of a bilingual latino play about families and AIDS titled *I Always Meant to Tell You...But*. She also serves as Southern California's Regional Director of Cornell's Black Alumni Association and is in the Empowerment Program for "Women in Films." It is WIF's goal, as it is with Angel Harper, to encourage every young girl to seek her full potential.

DR. ED HIBLER

34 Sex, Sin, and Satisfaction in the Classroom
by Ed Hibler, Ed.D.

As a psychologist and educator at California State University Fresno, I was a founding professor of the Human Sexuality classes and Sex Counseling for graduate students working for their doctorates in psychology.

I quickly discovered that there was—and still is—an appalling void in general knowledge about sexuality among people of all ages, not just the active and lusty young, despite an avalanche of printed materials, audio and video tapes on every conceivable aspect of human sexuality.

My students usually ranged in age from teens to 60, with one woman in my evening class who was over 80. About half were married or living together; the rest were never-married, divorced or widowed.

To avoid possible embarrassment, I asked students to write their questions anonymously, and that they identify only their age, gender, and marital status.

My favorite question of all, and one I couldn't adequately answer of course, was: *"Don't you think they should lower the age of puberty?"*

(Q) *How effective are aphrodisiacs?*

This is a term taken from the name of the ancient Greek goddess of love, Aphrodite. Every culture on earth claims they have a drug, herb, animal part or potion that stimulates desire (oysters, rhino tusks, Spanish fly, etc.). The straight answer is that none are effective, they only may have a placebo effect due to people wanting to believe—and placebos, or inert sugar pills, are in reality very powerful convincers.

If I were to tell you I had discovered that rice, browned with a mixture of castor oil and seaweed, would turn you on, and if I were to peddle the recipe, assuring everyone that money would come rolling in—until the reports came in that users of this so-called magic potion were subsequently puking away their libido, the gullible would flock either to invest or to consume.

Trying to find some magic elixir which, when either eaten or drunk, would enhance sexual desire and/or performance, has been the goal of countless humans for centuries, mostly men in their declining years, not unlike the search for the fabled "Fountain of Youth." Yet we still don't have anything that's a sure thing, or even close to it.

The poor rhinocerous has been hunted to near extinction because millions of Asian men believe its horn, when powdered and ingested, will turn them on. There are two possible origins for the slang term "horny." One could be from the use of the rhino's tusk; the other could be from the many stories of overstimulated, love-starved sailors having spent the better part of a year cooped up in a tiny ship full of men going around the "horn" of South America and landing in Hawaii, desperately in search of women.

Indeed, the best aphrodisiac is a body that's well rested and nourished, and not constantly assaulted with insults like tobacco, booze, drugs or fatigue.

Is it true our desire decreases as we get older?

It's true. However, before breaking into tears let me remind you that desire continues throughout life or at least until some illness or injury destroys it. With the help and interest of a loving partner it can continue until death. Actually, many people lose that youthful, compelling, driving need of youth by the time they reach their seventies, sometimes much sooner. Obviously, sickness or substance abuse can also short-circuit the whole process.

One of the discoveries of the famed team of Masters and Johnson, sex researchers of the '70s, was that elderly people as a group do not become sexless dried-up creatures. With good health and interested partners, their sex life, however diminished, should remain with them until the end.

Q: *Has the sexual revolution caused much damage?*

The changes we see in the frankness and greater honesty in discussing intimate problems have been a plus, especially for women held in social bondage in a male-dominated society for centuries by ignorance and old traditions.

As with most dramatic social changes, however, some people seem to be compelled to test the limits of new attitudes for their own gratification, with the result that our media today are filled with a tawdry exploitation of sex, sickening and explicit sexual violence, and what appears to be a total abandonment of basic human decency. The desire to "sell" can often push the message into questionable areas of influence and suggestion before an emotionally unstable public.

There never has been a new movement or invention that ever escaped the experimentation of the creative, for good *or* evil.

Q: *Why do men feel threatened by powerful women?*

With a world emerging from centuries of male dominance, Kate Millett, author of *Sexual Politics*, said, "What goes largely unexamined, often even unacknowledged in our present social order, is the birthright priority whereby males rule females—military, industry, technology, universities, science, political office, and finance, in short, every avenue of power, including coercive police power, has been entirely in male hands. Even the Deity is male."

With such overpowering control and tradition, whenever a woman achieves some political power or some other formerly male level of authority, it makes some men [representing an exclusive club or the powers that be] uneasy, and a lot of them resort to public denigration and sneering remarks [to keep her in "her place"].

Our former president's wife, Hillary Rodham Clinton, a lawyer, and clearly one of the most able, articulate, and dynamic women in public life, took a terrible beating in the media from some male politicians and pundits, most of whom were arch conservatives who resented her prominence in areas and issues like health care, with the hope of denigrating her husband for their own and their party's political gain.

Q: *If we're in the age of equality, why has the divorce rate increased and the traditional family values broken down?*

Just within my lifetime I've witnessed such things as the amendment giving women the right to vote, openness about sexual behavior, fail-safe contraception, research to prove women have sexual needs similar to men, and other discoveries that have overturned long-standing misinformation about social behavior. All have had a profound effect on "traditional" family life.

Although women are still lagging behind men in compensation, there seems to be no area of endeavor where women are not as capable as men, be it in law, medicine, or the high ranks of business and industry.

The pressures created are inescapable. Never were they a factor in earlier times, when women were almost exclusively in a supportive and nurturing role in the family.

In the last 50 years television has also proven to be a family-splitting invention. Children have their own TV, and the family rarely gets together for meals or the chance to talk with one another except to say hello or wave goodbye.

Today's "average family" may be a single mother with dependent children, or a husband and wife both of whom work, with children who come home from school to little or no supervision.

Q: *What has been the single most significant event to advance the role of women in society?*

In my opinion it was the invention of "The Pill" as a nearly fail-safe contraceptive. It has freed women from being totally at the mercy of annual pregnancies, whether they wanted them or not. Then add the findings of recent research within the sexual sciences which finally give women, after centuries of ignorance about their own bodies and needs, confidence in themselves as real people, not just playthings or "gofers" for men.

Q: *How do you prevent your partner from losing interest?*

By paying loving attention to your spouse every day and every night, and generally acting like a friend. The question seems to have a wistful tone as if there is concern that something is lacking now that the honeymoon is over, and the glow may have worn off.

All young marrieds have a lot of anxiety and self doubts when they first walk down the matrimonial road. After all they haven't been there before. As Edgar Guest, that old-time poet used to say, "It takes a heap o' livin' to make a house a home." A lot of lovin,' too.

(Editor's note: Edgar Guest's contemporary and fellow poet Ogden Nash wrote a similar piece of intimate advice to the newlywed couple: "If you're wrong, admit it; if you're right, forget it."

Taking a cue from their style of writing, love is equalled only by a sense of humor and a lighthearted approach to everything. Only then will you both be easy to be with, keeping interest high within a relaxed and agreeable atmosphere of compatibility.)

PILAR McRAE

35 A Tree Grows in El Monte
by Pilar McRae

My first sight of that campus in El Monte, California, was appalling. Trash and graffiti were visible everywhere at the Kranz Middle School, and the impression was not an inviting one.

My reaction was not because I am an overly neat or fussy kind of individual. It came from the experience of knowing how this kind of an environment can affect the attitudes of the students and faculty.

Nothing is more destructive to motivation, which is the very essence of success and achievement, than to be surrounded by evidence of such carelessness and disrespect. As a teacher, I have always depended on the enthusiasm of my pupils.

I decided then that something should be done.

In my first meeting with the principal, I proposed a radical idea. I strongly suggested that the asphalt and concrete be removed, and that it all be replaced with trees and plants. The planting should be done by student volunteers, the plants paid for by donations from supportive merchants, or given to us by one of the local nurseries. I promised him great changes would take place, and that I was willing to coordinate the effort.

The idea seemed overwhelming to some of the more outspoken members of the staff and faculty, so I took the idea instead to the students themselves. In the less negative minds of the youth it seemed that all things were possible. I suggested that, with some effort, they could turn their campus into a showplace of pride instead of embarrassment. Their reaction was due to their young imaginations and a desire to enjoy school instead of wallowing in a dump of trash.

Slowly the students' attitude prevailed. We obtained the support of a local nursery. The reception by the owners and employees when the students visited was very warm. Students not only chose the trees and plants, but also learned about them from experts.

Soon the parents saw the difference in their children. They too started to become involved as volunteers. They were called "Club de Padres Voluntarios" (Volunteer Parents Club). I got a strong feeling we were underway as smiles began to replace expressions of indifference. Next, the faculty and staff caught the vision of what we were attempting to do, which created a greater unity between them and the youth. The total value raised for that first year was computed at $6,000 for volunteer effort (student and parents) and materials donated at $18,687.50 for a grand total of $24,687.50.

With our goal of planting 500 trees, we created the popular Kranz Planting Club. Membership could be earned only by achieving an acceptable academic level. As a result, the overall test scores of the entire school soared. The members wore specially designed uniforms with great pride. The Cougar symbol of the school and the words Kranz School were embroidered on their dark blue vests, and their matching caps had the word KRANZ above the visor.

We started with no money, no trees, and no tools. But we planted 1,047 trees on those three acres. Taking a cue from a Wanaque, New Jersey high school, our slogan was E.R.A.S.E. (End Racism and Sexism Everywhere) to motivate the voluntary graffiti removal. Then the school district repainted the entire school in blue and white.

A variety of flowers and vegetables, including tomatoes, chiles, zucchini, yellow squash, cucumbers and bell peppers, was given free-of-charge to the neighboring community who had been so supportive. They simply had to come and pick the vegetables when ready to harvest. Many of the homes around the school, inspired by our example and the dramatic change on the Kranz campus, emulated the tree, vegetable and floral garden planting on their own property.

We painted 34 trash cans with the motto "Keep Kranz Clean," in English, in Spanish, in Chinese and in Vietnamese. The students discovered the greatest lesson of all—that hard work is fun and creates friendships when people toil side by side in a common cause.

Not only had all the graffiti been removed, but all the benches and the borders around the planters were painted. We planted rye grass in the front of the school and had the school district install automatic sprinklers. Two greenhouses were built. An "Adopt-a-Tree" program raised $451 dollars. The *San Gabriel Valley Tribune* featured an article about us on May 7, 1994. Los Angeles Beautiful Incorporated gave us a "special" award at the Los Angeles Chamber of Commerce on June 2 of that year.

Then something quite special happened.

We received a letter from Mark Steele, Director of the Noxzema Extraordinary Teen Awards, saying, "Dear Mrs. McRae, We are delighted to inform you that the Kranz Planting Club has been selected as the Western Regional Finalist...in recognition of the group's outstanding volunteer effort. As a Regional Finalist, your school's group will receive a $2,500 grant...."

"You should take pride in the fact that your group was chosen as a Regional Finalist from over 1,300 entries for its extraordinary energy, enthusiasm and commitment to making a difference. We will be contacting you shortly to make arrangements for a group [of your students] and a school representative to travel to New York, all expenses paid, for the Grand Prize competition [$10,000]."

It's important to note that Kranz was one of five top finalists nationwide, the only intermediate school with four senior high schools, which gave Kranz a three-year age *dis*advantage. Under the circumstances, just being chosen was a remarkable honor.

We were national finalists, from a school that a few years before was at the bottom academically, and a neighborhood disgrace. Even more important were the inner feelings of pride that grew among the students, and their desire to make a difference in their school, their community, and their life.

JOHN ERNST

John G. Ernst was born in Saskatoon, Canada, to an American father and an English mother. In May of 1941, he joined the U.S. Marine Corps in Seattle and attended "Boot Camp" at Camp Pendleton in California. He was assigned to a Marine Corps Fighter Squadron and, after two trips to the South Pacific and a short stay in the "Good Old USA," he left the Corps in 1945. In 1946 he applied and was accepted by the Los Angeles Police Department.

Following his retirement from the Police Department, he continued his membership with the Hollywood Coordinating Council, was a member of the American Cancer Society, and also served two terms as the President of the Executive Toastmasters Club of Glendale, California.

36 Dumb-Duh-Dumb-Dumb!
by John Ernst

In the criminal justice system you will find people who can be *really* dumb.

Let's take, for example, the victim. LAPD received a call indicating domestic violence from the neighbors of a couple who had had problems before. Apparently *she* was the abusive one in this altercation which had occured in the late afternoon.

When the officers interviewed them, he was at a loss to be able to explain, to either his wife or to the police, what had happened. He had been walking out of the grocery store when the bottom of his paper sack broke open, emptying the food onto the sidewalk and into the gutter. "At that moment a young lady, leaving the gym next door, ran over to help me," he said. "She had a plastic sack in her hand and offered to let me use it to repack the groceries I was picking up off the sidewalk and street."

The wife's expression reflected disbelief.

"I didn't notice anything else was already in the sack. We just stuffed the food in it, I thanked her, and I left for home with the sack in the back of my car. How could I know that there was a pair of women's panties in the bottom of it? It was full of food when she handed it to me."

When they examined the garment in question, it was wet. The girl must have taken a change of underwear with her to the gym, changed into dry panties, and dropped the wet ones into the bag after her swim.

"I swear, Honey, I never saw the girl before in my life."

* * *

The petty criminal is often lacking quite a few brain cells. There was a lady shopping with her baby at a very expensive boutique in Beverly Hills. She entered a changing room and, after using it to change into her new blouse, she then changed her baby's very messy diaper. She deposited the smelly mess into the elegantly decorated paper bag from the store, picked it up, paid for the new blouse and began walking out of the store with the baby in her arms.

When she was halfway across the floor heading for the exit of the boutique, a man who had been stalking the area for likely victims who might be carrying expensive merchandise, jumped out from behind a rack of clothes. He grabbed the store's paper bag out of her hand and darted out of the door. Since it was in a large mall, the management quickly called security and they nabbed the thief before he got to the main exit.

When the police arrived, the expressions on the faces of the thief and the security guard graphically reflected the "treasure" found inside the customer's bag. The guard had reluctantly fished around the bottom of the bag and found a credit card receipt revealing the name of the customer. Since he already knew the location of the store by the name on the bag, he had no problem returning the perpetrator to the scene of the crime.

They took this petty thief and the "evidence" into custody, and the customer was very happy to release the stolen items for use in the prosecution.

* * *

During the Rodney King riots in Los Angeles in 1992, passions ran wild following the jury verdict acquitting the four policemen. They were attempting to arrest Rodney King after he failed to stop for a traffic violation, which required that the officers pursue him in a dangerously high speed chase through residential streets. When he finally stopped he resisted arrest. The officers attempted to control him which caused many people to believe, due to a videotape of the incident, that this allegedly brought the full force of police brutality on the head of Rodney King. Had he stopped like most people do, we would never have had the publicity, the riot, nor would we have known the name of Rodney King.

They interviewed an elderly lady who found herself in the wrong place at the wrong time, and who had been verbally attacked by a group of young people from the black community. Some people with white skin became temporary victims in the heat of the moment.

As she stood back against the wall, her quick thinking and her words possibly saved her life by reversing the situation.

Slightly bending the truth she shouted at them, "I was with Martin Luther King, the champion of NON-VIOLENCE! I was there marching across the Edmund Pettis Bridge in Selma, Alabama almost 40 years ago with a thousand other supporters of civil rights—and many of us were *white!*

"Reverend King would be ashamed of all of you if he was here right now. So back off and remember *what* we are ALL fighting for!" she yelled.

They quietly apologized, turned and ran away.

* * *

During the O.J. Simpson trial many of the curious people in the community drove to his home, the site of the murders, to see the area for themselves. Two ladies, one of them nearly ninety years old and her daughter who was driving, got in line with several other slow-moving cars full of similarly gawking people. When the police tried to re-direct traffic there was some confusion, and the daughter, attempting to turn around, backed into a temporary fence set up around the property near O.J.'s estate. She knocked it over! In a panic she sped away down a side street, only to be stopped by a barracading police car.

Angrily ordered out of the car, the daughter was taken to the police vehicle and made to sit in the rear seat with two "interviewing" officers. During the mock shakedown of the daughter, several other officers looked in on her 90-year-old mother to see if she was all right.

The officers quickly realized that it was only the daughter's innocent panic that sent her speeding down the street. Nonetheless, they decided to teach this "looky-lou" a lesson. They each tried valiantly to keep a straight face throughout the so-called interrogation interview.

"You have the right to remain silent. If you give up that right...." She immediately started crying, visualizing the cold, gray walls of a cell in the Sybil Brand Institute for Women. They continued melodramatically, "You aren't planning to leave town, are you? I must have your phone number for my report. Are you ready to answer questions if called on?"

With a few more questions, they were of the opinion she was sufficiently remorseful and let her go. In the midst of an otherwise tense and confusing afternoon, the police assumed they had left a lasting impression on her while enjoying a moment of diversion.

* * *

In a similar situation, the police misdirected two elderly but inquisitive ladies who had told their family they were going to attend a Gay Pride Parade as spectators—out of curiosity! Attempting to park the car, they misinterpreted the directions of the police and they found themselves, not in a parking lot, but instead on *the main downtown boulevard—near the head of the parade!*

They were suddenly crowded among brightly decorated vehicles—and *people*. They tried desperately to attract the attention of the next traffic officer, waving their arms out the window to an enthusiastic crowd who returned their waves. They found out the next day, after receiving numerous phone calls, that several members of their family, friends and neighbors had observed the whole thing on the local evening television news.

Years later, they told us their accidental celebrity status remained unforgettable, and an unending topic of conversation among their many delighted friends.

DR. ED HIBLER

37 Oh, Those Gutsy Geezers!
by Ed Hibler, Ed.D., and Jackie Hibler

The papers today are full of family disaster stories: both husband and wife working for years expecting to quit early with full retirement. Now he's had a stroke and she has to quit to care for him. They're both out of work and no income. Or he's been with an international conglomerate his entire working life. Now the company's downsizing and he's out on his ear just two months before retirement.

The stories are endless; the tragedies multiply.

Now we had our own.

I was a former advertising and sales executive and later a college psychology professor and licensed psychotherapist; my wife Jackie had been a special education teacher, educational therapist, and former executive director of a local chapter of a large public health agency.

We had worked out a simple plan for retirement. I would teach till age 63, then take early retirement. Jackie would retire from the classroom at the same time, and both of us would then spend full time on our respective counseling practices which had previously been part-time; then we'd retire, permanently, within five years. So far so good.

To help reorganize our finances for these things, after what we assumed was careful planning, we decided to sell our big country dream house we had lovingly built eight years earlier, buy a much smaller place, invest the difference, and travel.

Then everything blew!

To shorten an appalling four-year story, we sold and got back the big house four times due to circumstances we could not possibly have anticipated. On the strength of a small deposit with the first contract of sale, we had bought a charming, though much smaller modular home in the Sierra foothill gold-rush country, planning to pay it off when the sale of the large home was concluded. We were ecstatic until a phone call two weeks after the deposit had been made, informed us our buyers had had a head-on collision. They survived, but were so badly hurt they were forced to back out of the deal. Now Jackie and I had two substantial house payments to make out of an already drastically reduced retirement income.

Subsequently, in a dormant real estate market, we resold the place three more times on lease option contracts over the next four years. There were long periods with the house empty and deteriorating, with no income to carry its costs. Each "sale" was at a lower price, plus the extensive damage to the house by one of our "buyers." Lawsuits against buyers who defaulted on their contracts, then declared bankruptcy, cost us thousands more.

We were faced with the bitter reality of losing the smaller house, and having to go to work—somewhere, somehow—again.

One night we sat at our dining room table, desperately trying to figure a way out of financial disaster. Going back to teaching was out, except for perhaps an occasional fill-in job. Reopening our practices would cost thousands we didn't have to organize and relocate, and then several years to rebuild.

Because of our ages—Jackie was 60 and I was 70—we felt we were beyond all that. We needed to find something that could bring in at least part of what we had lost, and do it quickly! But who would hire a couple of old geezers like us, especially professional geezers? No time to start over. Prospects were grim.

Fate flicked a fickle finger with a ringing doorbell.

There at our door stood two old friends we hadn't seen in ages, Joan and Bob Renney. We had corresponded occasionally, but this was our first face-to-face meeting in many years.

Vivacious Joan, petite and blonde with a touch of silver, was in her sixties. Husband Bob, about the same age, a retired university professor like me, towered over her. He wore a thick, wavy mane of silver hair topping a smiling weathered and deeply lined face.

The four of us quickly gathered around our table for dinner and an excited and animated recap of our lost years. When we were up to date on our respective lives, Jackie and I poured out our financial anguish and fears.

Bob listened intently, then said, "Hey, why don't you guys do what *we've* been doing for five years? You can wipe out that debt, and I can help you get started." Joan was a former Junior Leaguer with Jackie. Joan had graduated from a prestigious California women's college, had earned a graduate degree in Cordon Bleu cooking, had been an executive chef and later had managed a private, very posh recreational facility before meeting Bob. Bob had been a botanist and professor of natural sciences at an eastern university. Both had sworn they would never again live in what they called "genteel poverty," since their respective divorces. But what they had both been doing to avoid that fate fascinated us.

After first doing some clever research, they decided that if they couldn't live like millionaires, then they would move to an area where lots of them resided—and go to work for them. They discovered by using live-in quarters with virtually all living expenses covered, and saving nearly all of their substantial salaries, they could lay aside $40,000 to $50,000 a year, enough to later set themselves up in their own catering and/or consultant business without borrowing money.

They decided to look for employment with Joan as caretaker-cook-consultant to wealthy landowners in California's lush wine-growing region of Napa Valley, north of San Francisco Bay.

They had been doing this now for five years, with a super-wealthy family with multiple homes around the country, a fleet of expensive cars, a private jet and helicopter, acres of vineyards and orchards surrounding the home where they now worked.

Joan took care of the huge mansion while Bob oversaw all the maintenance and landscaping, doubling as butler during rare weekend parties. "It's a lush paradise, and our employers are rarely there, except on an occasional weekend. Don't tell us you can't do it.

"Moneyed people have a devil of a time finding and keeping reliable help. Your greatest assets are your honesty and integrity. You'll live like millionaires. You're naturals for this kind of a situation."

With virtually nothing to lose, at breakfast the next morning we told Joan and Bob we'd give it a try.

"You won't regret it, guys," yelled Bob, waving as he backed their Lexus out of our driveway.

On our way back to the house, Jackie commented wistfully, "I always thought by the time I'd reached this age I'd *have* a cleaning lady, not *be* one."

But before we had a chance to hear from Joan and Bob, an ad appeared in a bay area paper asking for "a mature couple" to help manage a large new residence for well-to-do retirees. We decided to apply and were accepted.

We were now the totally inexperienced co-managers of The Lingerwood Retirement Residence, with 92 residents, all supposedly ambulatory. We arranged to have our home cared for, mail forwarded, lawn mowed, etc.

Imagine, if you can, being in charge of a 97-room elegant mansion with 92 elderly children, plus 12 teenagers who served the meals, five housekeepers, a van driver and two gardeners, and you may have an idea of some of the craziness that lay before us. Add a coffee machine that constantly broke down, overflowing on our shoes and all over the carpeting, an irritable copy machine that screwed up regularly, and an electric typewriter that unpredictably skipped and jumped across the page, and you know only a small part of it.

The first morning the second floor clothes dryer caught on fire, and the washer on the third floor flooded. The first few days we were working 14-hour days just to stay ahead.

Strangely, one of our wishes was to be able to take time to get to know the residents better. One was an ex-opera singer, another a well known surgeon, another an author and artist, and several were retired military, with one general and one admiral aboard.

But there was one who was able to sum it all up in delightful verse. Lucie Harrison had become the facility's resident poet and storyteller at the age of 88, and she had had a half dozen of her books of lighthearted poetry published, She was writing another based on her experiences at Lingerwood. She called one of them "Grumble Bees."

Grumble Bees

I've uncovered one thing
Down through the years,
Some folks are hard to please.
So, inventing a name
For those chronic complainers,
I'll call them "Grumble Bees."

When people are young
They want to be old;
Dieters, in a class by themselves.
Where to begin
With the ones who are thin
The fat ones all want to be elves.

The thin ones all stuff
Much more than enough,
And the fat ones all starve to be thin.
The blondes and brunettes,
Are continually swapping,
The color of each other's hair...

That was only a part of it. Lucie helped all of us keep everything in perspective.

JUDITH (CHASE) JEFFERIES

38 "Go For It"

by Judith (Chase) Jefferies

I had my first love affair when I was about eight years old. Our school class visited a quaint little white house, which in our small town was the local library. It reminded me of a cozy cottage. Once I saw those rows and rows of books, I was hooked. To me, learning has always equaled success.

Early in life, I learned a variety of meanings when someone spoke of success. Mine was defined that day in the library. When hopes to further my education in the traditional manner could not be realized, I knew I had to develop a different plan for learning. This plan took many forms and was met with a multitude of challenges.

I grew up on a dairy farm near the small town of North Fairfield, Ohio. My parents, also from farming communities, were children of the Great Depression of the Thirties. Our way of life was modest, but we never went without. Because of life's circumstances, my parents had limited access to higher education, and as far as I know, didn't aspire for more. They seemed reconciled and happy with their lifestyle, which was one of hard work. In turn, they taught my siblings and me a strong work ethic, for which I have always been grateful.

However, the more I learned in school, the more I wanted to learn and grow. When I began to speak of aspirations beyond what we had, I was met with skepticism and resistance.

"Why would you want to know about different parts of the world and other lifestyles?" a friend asked. "Isn't what we have here good enough for you?" I winced at the hurt in her voice.

"Of course it is," I said. But I wanted to know more, needed to know more.

I wouldn't trade my wonderful childhood for anything. What I had on the farm is the very essence of who I am.

But we weren't totally isolated.

Movies and television provided the stimulus to consider other possibilities. Newsrooms, hospital environments, and the excitement of courtrooms fascinated me.

After milking cows, baling hay and slopping hogs, I found the idea of broadening my horizons compelling.

At home, I was taught valuable lessons by being expected to do many things an adult would do, even though I was a child.

In a single day, I cooked for a threshing crew, did the dishes and returned to the fields to help bale hay.

On another day, I mowed a front lawn, a back yard, a side yard and a grove. The only lawnmower I had was one I pushed. I was ten years old. I didn't consider it burdensome—just a way of life.

Even with all the work, we still found time for fun. Like the day my neighbor friend, Jeannie, and I decided to drag race our orange-yellow Minneapolis Moline tractors down our country road. We had a great time skidding around in the dirt. The billowing clouds of dust drew the curious to come and see the spectacle we were making of ourselves. When my dad found out, movies and television were out of the question for a period of time. But to this day it is one of my fondest memories.

One time some city kids thought they were being clever by letting our goats out of their pen. To our delight, the goats chased them all over the neighborhood.

Another visiting city boy whined and demanded to ride the pony he saw out in the field.

Finally, tired of his demands, we said, "Go ahead. Ride it."

Mom ran out of the house wanting to know why Johnny was trying to ride a bull calf.

In time, we grew to laugh with each other and understood what Andrew Carnegie meant when he said, *"There is little success where there is little laughter."*

When I was suddenly uprooted from that wonderful and beloved farm to a smaller farm several miles to the east, I knew I faced a new challenge. I resisted the school as much as I had the move. But here I met the teacher who made a dramatic impact on my life.

Learning had an exciting new meaning. The teacher, Rod Righter, urged me to work hard in every subject. Schoolwork became fun. I especially loved English. The written word became paramount to me and from then on I relished writing the essays and reports assigned to us in class. I was encouraged by my teachers to keep writing. I loved books and through them learned of other worlds and avenues to them.

Mr. Righter showed me he had faith in my abilities and in me. Along with my parents, he helped instill understanding of how character and integrity would affect everything I would ever do in life.

He taught me to be responsible by trusting me with a classroom of children when a teacher needed to be away for a short time. He allowed me to go into areas of the school usually off limits to students. Eventually, I babysat his three beautiful daughters and enjoyed reading stories to them before bedtime. He involved me in performances where I played my accordion, one of the most important for me being our eighth grade graduation. I don't know where I got the courage to perform, but I think mostly it had to do with his faith in me. I didn't want to let him down.

I learned at the age of fourteen what mentors are, how valuable they are in life, and how vital it is to have someone who encourages you to get past those who say, "You can't do it."

Several years later, when I was a desperate young divorcée with a small daughter to support, an uncle made a suggestion. He was sure I would enjoy legal work and said it would challenge me. I told him most of the legal jobs in our small town were already taken and no law office was advertising for help.

He said, "Go ahead anyway. You can do this. The worst that can happen is you will get a 'No'."

Totally inexperienced, I felt awkward and didn't know what to say or do.

With a little coaching, I followed his suggestion.

I approached a law office and said to one of the partners, "I heard perhaps you could use some part-time help. You have an excellent reputation and I would like to work for you."

To my surprise, he said, "Yes," and I learned one of the most valuable lessons of my life. *If you want something—go for it.* I began working part-time for one attorney and in a matter of a few months was working part-time for two additional attorneys. These experiences provided me with enough courage to come to Southern California to look for better opportunities.

Once in California, I found an excellent government position, which required a top-secret clearance. I was very young for such responsibilities, but my past experiences, school records and excellent recommendations helped me to secure the job.

One day I was called to the personnel office. I trembled as I inched my way down long corridors. In this city far from home, I desperately needed the job to support my daughter and myself.

"You wanted to see me?" I asked.

The personnel manager said, "Yes, I wanted to meet the one who got three excellent recommendations. I've never seen this before."

He showed me the letters he had received from my former employers back home. I was very touched by these heartfelt comments from people I had faithfully worked for. They reinforced my absolute belief that doing my best and doing the right thing were the only ways to succeed. I was doing what I once thought—and had been told—I couldn't do. I was learning, and I wanted to educate myself more.

A friend told me about another wonderful opportunity in Southern California. A chance to attend college. I never thought it would be possible as my funds were so limited. But I moved to a city with a community college. Books were my only expense.

"Enroll," she said. I was a girl from a farm in the Midwest, unaware of even how to search out the many opportunities all about me.

I enrolled.

I had only one required class to complete for Chiropractic College when I lost my mother to cancer.

Immediately following, I developed serious back problems and was unable to continue my education. But I had learned—when one plan isn't possible, make another.

I did, and worked with some of the most successful attorneys in Los Angeles. I enjoyed the legal life and learned greatly from it, but I had never lost my interest in medicine.

So when I learned of an excellent opportunity to work in the medical field for the administrator of a hospital, I applied for and got the job—an exciting new chapter in my life, which I loved. I remained in that field for many years.

Writing for publication was something I seriously considered after I returned to college and studied creative writing. An added course through the UCLA extension program inspired even more dedication.

I eventually joined a writer's group where their enthusiasm, drive, attitude and outlook stimulated and encouraged me.

My quantity of writing has been interrupted too frequently by "have to" situations in life, but I have succeeded in having a number of things published. The harder I work, the greater are the rewards. With other restraints removed, to enroll in more classes is now also possible. *"It's never too late."*

The most important thing I've learned is never to give up, and to keep challenging myself. I believe the best path to success is to associate with positive, uplifting, successful people—and to laugh. As e e cummings said, *"The most wasted of all days is one without laughter."*

I went past the pessimists, the people who tried to make me think I could never realize my dreams. They could not drag me down, destroy my faith in the future or myself.

As for back home, when I visit, I always go by the little quaint cottage where my love for books began—and smile.

This used to be the library. It is now a museum. Picture courtesy of the North Fairfield Firelands Historical Assn. (1959)

Roderic E. Righter and Judith I. Chase.

WILLIAM DERRINGER

Bill Derringer's plays have had the continual distinction of being presented on both coasts and throughout the country. He has been a produced playwright for more than 25 years. 2003 has seen the NOHO Jewish Theatre League's production of his short play *Shiva Warriors* at the Bitter Truth in North Hollywood. At the start of 2002, his one act play *Back to Back* was chosen by the Pennsylvania Playhouse for their Tenth Annual One-Act Playwriting Competition. His short comedy *Destiny's Roommate* had its California premiere in the Bitter Truth's First Annual One Act Play Festival—and also *Doctor On Call* had its premiere as part of the Palm Springs National Short Play Fest 2002.

Bill was chosen as the National Theatre Judge for the 2002 Porter Fleming Writing Competition sponsored by the Greater Augusta GA Arts Council.

39 My Bubba's Weekly Meeting
by William Derringer

Saturday, her big day. The children are coming and she must get ready. The kasha and the knishes and the hot soup were being prepared. The kitchen was her place, her life. She busied herself at the stove as she adjusted a schemata rag tied around her head. The rag was to relieve the headaches of responsibility and old age. Her plain print dress that she had purchased on Ninth Street and the black heavy shoes that she had owned for years were her proper Saturday night gathering dress.

Bubba had the magnificent beauty that has remained with her since her youth. She was strong peasant stock. The gray hair pushed back into a bun couldn't hide the radiant eyes that possessed the wisdom and strength to hold together a family. Her four gorgeous daughters she called her chicks. It was 1949, and I was still as Bubba said "A pitzala...a baby." I thought she was so terrific. I still do.

She knew her children well. Lately she had some doubts though. Maybe they were starting to.... The doorbell rang.... "Ruthie," she yelled, "get the door, it's your sisters." Ruth was upstairs dressing when the bell rang. She was afraid to open the door and let them in. When she did open the door they would only remind her that she was single and alone.

It was about time she got married and why not Lillian's husband Meyer's brother Bernie. He was a perfect match. It didn't matter how she felt about it, the family had decided her fate and she was expected to carry it through. She thought a moment about Bernie. What's so bad? she thought. He was nice, kind—not her idea of romantic but she wasn't exactly a glamour girl. She had to admit she was tired and scared of being alone. How many more years could she take the words of Auntie Ruth without running out of the room in tears? Another knock. It was them! Family never gives up. Never goes home.

Ruth walked down the stairway to go to the door and as she did she glanced at the things now so everyday in her life. The long sofa, well worn and covered with those lace doilies that were on the sofa arms to hide its age. The huge dining room chifforobe and the plastic tablecloth blending in with the flowered wallpaper. There was the picture of my Bubba and her deceased beloved husband who was so handsome looking and romantic. She called him a *goniff* because he stole her heart away.

Did you know I was named after him? The first named too. She told me many times I had his good looks and charm. Those good looks and charm trapped Bubba into a marriage of struggle and poverty. To win her, he pretended to be a rich American. He swept her off her feet by all of his talk and dreams. What a dreamer!

If that wasn't bad enough, with the waiting and traveling on the boat to the new country, Sarah found out she was carrying her first chick. So she tells him she's pregnant and he tells her that he's poor. What could they do but face the truth, kiss and love and struggle together. They had very little money to offer their babies but they gave them the riches of love, kindness and humor.

Ruth opened the door, but standing there at the doorway was not her sisters, but old and frail Ruchel, Bubba's girlhood friend. They had both arrived here from the old country those many years ago. Ruchel smiled weakly and said "Ruthie, I'm sorry to bother you because I know it's after Shabbos dinner and the weekly meeting, but I wondered if Sarah could spare some fish and some horseradish." Ruth beckoned her. "Let me tell you, Ruthie, don't get hooked up with a bricklayer like my Edna." I told her he was a good for nothing, but does she ever listen? Such a cheat. Find yourself a nice steady man who doesn't cheat. He works, comes home and sleeps, someone you can count on. If my Bennie were alive to see her tears, he would die all over again."

Bubba then walked in slightly flustered when she saw Ruchel. But, as always, Bubba half listened to Edna's tales of woe. As Ruchel spoke, Bubba would think about her own chicks. All those years they hung onto her apron strings and she'd hug and kiss away all their troubles. She was always there for them. To listen to them, to offer a tissue when they'd cry, to offer a buck if they needed it. Always to tell them when they were acting like a jackass. They knew mom didn't lie. Ruchel's complaining was always soothing to Bubba. Bubba would think about the chicks growing up. The joy of seeing them go to school and grow up to be healthy young ladies.

Ruthie was her treasure. Out of all of them, Ruthie was the smartest, the gentlest and the one with honesty and inner beauty. Bubba Sarah could not leave this world without her Ruthie having a nice and decent husband. Her Ruthie—a bride.

Ruchel and Sarah were so close they were almost one. Now when their children had grown they were growing old together. "Come, Ruchel, I'll give you fish, a knish and how about some borsht?" Sarah said. "It will do you good." They both went into the kitchen as Ruth started to straighten the pillows on the sofa. She thought again of Bernie. If only Bernie weren't so shy and if she wasn't so scared. Maybe it wouldn't be so bad the two of them. He's sweet she thought. If only....

The doorbell rang and Ruth froze in place. It was them. Another Saturday trapped. Oh well! She opened the door. Lillian swept into the room, all smiles as she modeled her new mink coat. "Ruthie, you like?" Ruth stared down at the mink. "It's lovely Lil, but doesn't Estelle have one too?" "Oh please Ruth, do you know what this one cost. It's so much nicer." Meyer gave it to me last week for our anniversary. It's something, huh? Now would Estelle's Sol give her something like this? The man's filthy rich but so stingy. My Meyer wants me to have things with quality. You...you need to get married."

Back in the kitchen Bubba was pouring some hot soup into a small pot for Ruchel to take home with her. "Ruchel, before you go, I have something I must tell you. You got to promise you won't cry and you won't faint." Ruchel looked at her with panic in her eyes. "Oh Sarah.... Oh my God what is it? You're not leaving me. Don't tell me, I don't want to hear. My best friend. My only friend. God take me. I have no life. My daughter won't talk to me. I'm a sour, bitter person. Sarah you can't die. Take me God—please."

Bubba put her hand on Ruchel's mouth. "Ruchel sha! Who

said I was going to die? The doctor said maybe. But you know he's been telling me that for twenty years. He thinks I work too much, I worry too much. This is true." Ruchel looked at Bubba curiously. "Then why are you scaring me? I'm ready to give myself to God in your place and you tell me it's a maybe. Keep your soup. I'm going home."

Bubba patted Ruchel's head. "Ruchel, I got a question for you." Ruchel looked at her defiantly. "I'm not going to listen to another word." Bubba tried to soothe her. "But if I were, would you take care of my chicks for me? Only you I trust." Ruchel looked surprised. "Who me? Your chicks are old hens already. They should take care of themselves." Sarah smiled. "If I did would..." Ruchel was exasperated. "Yes, Sarah, I would. As much as I could, I would." Bubba kissed her on the cheek. "Thank you, that's all I had to hear."

The living room was filled now with Sarah's chicks, well almost all her daughters were present. There were yells toward the kitchen for Sarah to come join them, but not now. She was too busy in the kitchen pouring out her heart and gathering her thoughts. "Ruchel, whatever happens, don't say a word to my children. Only you and me know. Is that a promise?" Ruchel was confused. "Whatever you say."

As Ruchel started to leave Bubba added, "You know, Ruchel, I think today is going to be the most important meeting me and my chicks ever had." They must fly on their own. You my friend...you know what I mean. She hugged her friend. "Thank you. I love you."

In the living room Shirley, the eldest was sitting legs apart, smoking feverishly, and going into the "why don't you marry Bernie, Ruth?" Ruth was cringing in the chair next to the living room door and Herschel, Shirley's husband, a neatnik, was going around the room cleaning out the ashtrays. He ceased doing this at Shirley's command and took his seat beside her. Now everyone was in the living room awaiting the last member of the family. She preferred it this way. Estelle finally arrived, mink stole and all, but to her surprise she saw Lillian's new mink hanging up in the hallway. She entered the living room less magnificently than usual. Lillian was thrilled; she had won their constant competition.

As Sarah entered the living room she instantly sized up everything. These weren't the young chicks that she raised with love and humor. They had changed and not for the better. Did they forget the struggles, the dreams, the caring for each other? After all these years, how could she not have seen this sooner? The changes happening bit by bit.

Walking into that room was now an awakening for her. What she saw was a nest full of strangers. All of them going in different directions. How did this happen? How did the family get so lost? So divided. Well it must stop and right now! She thought, "I must do something."

She silently prayed for the strength, the knowledge. The sweet love of my grandfather to guide her towards the next thought, her next move. This will be a meeting my chicks will never forget. It has to work. She took her time strolling over to the sofa all eyes following each move she made. What's mom up to, the chicks were thinking? She sat down slowly as she arranged the schemata on her forehead and with careful and loving words started to leave them with the only legacy she could.

From the heart, from the soul Sarah spoke. This was the last time my Bubba had a chance to pass on to her chicks all the goodness she had within her.

ESTHER PEARLMAN

Esther Pearlman has shown her art in numerous California exhibits. She illustrated and co-authored, with Melody Girard, *The Childrens Question Book*, Vol. I, *Oh Canada, Someone I Love Is in the Hospital*, and a forthcoming book that will be a tour of France. She lives in Santa Monica with her husband.
Email: estherpearlman@yahoo.com.

40 **My Bodyguard**
by Esther Pearlman

I couldn't have felt more out of place as a child if I had been abducted by aliens and dropped down in South Los Angeles. Like us, our immediate neighbors and my classmates were from lower middle class families who struggled and hoped for their piece of the American dream. Looking back, I realize that many of their parents were probably dustbowl refugees or immigrants. But to me all the kids belonged to an exclusive club, while I felt out of place.

My parents were immigrants from the Greek Island of Rhodes. This set me apart from my schoolmates, who wouldn't have known the Isle of Rhodes from Rhode Island. Making me feel even stranger, my parents spoke Ladino, the 15th Century Spanish of Jews who had been expelled from Spain in 1492. It's a language frozen in time, mixed with some Hebrew and sprinkled with language from the countries of refuge, such as Greece or Italy. Most of the English my parents knew, they learned from movies. My siblings and I assumed that our parents kept Ladino to themselves so they could have secrets from us.

Because I was behind in my language comprehension skills, I was held back in kindergarten. The teacher disciplined me often for failing to understand her instructions. Once, I accepted help from other kids. Angry, the teacher yelled and slapped my face, her open hand imprinting humiliation and the fear of teachers on me for many years to come.

We were about the only Jews still living in a rapidly transitioning neighborhood, bordered by Inglewood and Watts. The synagogues and their congregations had relocated to better parts of

Los Angeles. We couldn't afford to follow or pay synagogue fees, so we didn't have ready access to the social support of the Jewish community.

My mother was raised Orthodox; she finished each meal with a prayer. I think she longed for a kindred community. She looked sad many times. Smoking lifted her spirits and she smoked constantly, as did my father. Halos of smoke encircled them both most of the time. My father didn't talk much, but he whistled. After a long day at his little grocery store in Watts, he'd drive up honking his truck horn. He would then walk into the kitchen whistling and carrying a watermelon on his shoulder, like a porter in a third world farmers' market.

Dad's grocery store barely earned a subsistence income for his family of four children. He gave credit to people who couldn't pay their bills, even though we sometimes couldn't pay ours. More than once, the power or the phone company disconnected our service. Pain from ulcers and severe tooth decay robbed my father of many of life's joys. Eventually, frequent armed robberies, debt and poor health forced him out of business. Fortunately, he had let go of the store long before it burned down in the Watts riots in 1963.

After I had married and moved away, black folks in the old neighborhood used to slow down their cars and look at me when I came to visit my family. I'm ashamed to admit it, but the first time it happened, my heart pounded with fear as some men in a car cruised alongside me.

"Hey," a big man shouted at me, "Ain't you Jack's daughter? Jack that had the store on 103rd and Watts?"

"Yes," I replied, still not sure if I should answer.

"That Jack sure was a good man," the big man smiled. "Everyone loved him. Other storeowners, they was mean, but your daddy was generous."

After the store closed, my father worked as a deliveryman when his health permitted. My mother earned money caring for invalids, babysitting and selling flowers. After a long day, she would go into our kitchen and prepare delicacies so complex and sumptuous that it could have made a Greek restaurateur cry. With nimble fingers, she made delicate pastelicos—light little pastries packed with ground beef and rice, savory vegetables, hearty spanakopeta—like burikitas and bowikos—spinach and cheese pie, and sweet desserts wrapped in flaky phyllo crust and drizzled with honey (baklava).

My mother made most of my clothes. Although she was an excellent seamstress, I had only a few of the styles popular in the fifties and early sixties. For a kid, clothes can help you fit in or make you an object of scorn.

Mom was very protective. I was sick a lot and she may have feared losing me. I was just skin and bones, shy and a target for bullies. Fortunately for me, in late grammar school, I meet my protector and mentor—Julie.

Julie was my hero. We were completely unalike. I was tall, timid and afraid of conflict and stepping out of line. She was stocky and self-confident, with a violent temper and a nose for trouble.

We were constant companions, going out for sports together and sleeping over at each other's houses. My mother made us matching outfits, which we liked to wear on the same day. Julie's family had fewer kids at home and could afford more fashionable clothes, so she loaned me her outfits occasionally. When I wore them to school, my classmates would compliment rather than ridicule me.

When one of the rough girls wanted to fight me, Julie had a talk with her. The bully didn't bother me again.

I suffered from what people today call a learning disability. I'm convinced these problems were related to my mother being in labor with me for three days. I tried to enter the world backward, or breech presentation, which I think could have caused oxygen deprivation. I had trouble with school studies. Julie coached me in history, drilling me so I could remember facts.

Julie encouraged me to join the police-sponsored club for underprivileged kids, which took us to summer camp. She developed rivalries with other girls at camp, and played pranks on our rivals which sometimes got us called to the administration office for a scolding. Because of her, I went out for one of the highest honors in the group, called OSO. Julie was already an OSO, and her moral support helped me endure the rather unpleasant hazing I had to go through to receive this honor, so we could be equals.

Her adventurous spirit lead me to places that I would not have ventured alone. At her insistence, I went to the Pike amusement park with her and other kids from our club. We rode 30 miles to Long Beach in the back of an open stake-bed truck.

Sailors crowded the Pike, looking to get drunk, tattooed and fixed up with girls. We were enticed by the thrills of the roller coaster, the Ferris wheel and other rides. Grotesque canvas posters and barkers for the "freak shows," fortune-tellers and tattoo parlors intrigued us. Above the din of the crowd and the hurdy-gurdy, we could hear the excited shrieks of riders descending on the roller coaster. From anywhere in the park you could hear the hysterical laugher amplified from the funhouse "fat lady," an animatronic giant that bent at the waist and laughed raucously. The Pike smelled of cotton candy, corn dogs, creosote and the Pacific Ocean. Corndogs on sticks hung like fringe from the awnings of fast food booths. We did meet some sailors, but we were just 12 years old.

Julie always said she wanted to be a nun. Instead, she married and had eight children. I asked her to be the maid of honor at my wedding, but she didn't feel up to walking down the aisle while very pregnant with her first child. On holidays and birthdays, we still get in touch. We saw each other at her tearful 60th birthday party. As the years and family responsibilities intervened, we drifted apart. But the example Julie set for me in my youth stayed with me for life. She dared me to reach beyond my initial self-expectations. Without her example, I might not have dared to go to college. In spite of learning difficulties and children at home, I kept taking classes. By the time I finished my bachelor's degree, I had been in school so long that the college janitor said he remembered me before my hair had turned gray!

With the promise of fun, Julie enticed me into novel experiences. With words of encouragement, she propelled me forth into new accomplishments. She convinced me that I was capable of meeting any challenge. I'm not saying that she made my life a cakewalk, but she taught me to persevere, even when my confidence faltered. With Julie as a role model, I made the best of life and I continue to push myself forward. She helped me to become a "mensch," and that, as they say, "ain't no chopped liver."

FRANK BECKER

41 The *Music Man* of Japan
by Frank Becker

I lived in Japan from 1968 to 1982 where I composed and recorded concert music, and also taught music courses in the Geneva-based Yokohama International School. We had Japanese, European, American and various other Asian students ages six through 19—from first grade through high school plus two years for British A and O level exams—a very interesting and varied group of young people.

The Japanese schools had a very exacting and closed curricula, so most of these students couldn't fit into their system. We taught them in English, but they also learned Japanese from the second grade and French from the fourth grade.

When I was interviewed for the job I was told that they had an orchestra, a wind ensemble, instruments, facilities and everything I might need to teach. But when I started that following year I discovered there was no orchestra or wind ensemble, and one kid who owned a violin with only three strings. There was an old piano and a pile of poorly written books of folk tunes for little children—that was it!

"Where did everybody go?" I yelled out loud. I realized the so-called "music department" had been grossly exaggerated. This was an otherwise wonderful school of 400 well-behaved young people. The biggest problems we discussed at my first teachers' meeting were about kids who chew gum in class and how to teach first and second graders the locker combinations.

I raised my hand and said, "Why do you even *have* locks in this school? How do you teach sharing and respecting others' property if everything is locked up right from the beginning?"

"Let's take the locks off," everyone agreed. "They're a nuisance to maintain, and the students always lose the combinations anyway."

After studying all the available music texts, I decided to write them myself. By the time I left in the early '80s, we had acquired 21 synthesizers, video equipment, and we were doing all kinds of music projects. I had the whole school involved in making a film about how to read music. And we had fun with it.

Instead of the usual slogan for E-G-B-D-F (Every Good Boy Does Fine—lines of the treble clef), I suggested that they make up their own and film them as skits. One was "Every Girl Burps During French." So they filmed the fourth grade girls taking turns burping as the French teacher taught the class, including the kid in the back in a gorilla suit, who, in a later "slogan," represented the "G."

The spaces in the treble clef, F-A-C-E, were the faces of all the students, teachers and parents. The film showed a blank sheet of lined music paper with all these faces popping on, several per second, for about a minute. Then came a sequence of burping girls and all the other ideas they'd thought of. All the fun and effort reinforced not only the sequence of notes and how to read music, but also developed their film-making skills with stop-action animation, creative writing, acting, production, directing and working together.

From the beginning I taught all of them how to play keyboard with some using the piano, with others using paper keyboards and then switching to the piano so all could have the real experience. When I left years later, we had dozens of electronic keyboards with all of the students playing Bach and Bartok, right down the list of great composers. The serious study of music had become a riot of fun.

At certain holidays we would do concerts. I wrote musicals for these occasions and I would sneak in music lessons. For example, we did *Rumpelstiltskin*—only in my story Good King Irving had a favorite song, *Twinkle, Twinkle Little Star*. The Wicked Witch Who Wouldn't Brush Her Teeth cast an evil spell so no one would know how it went.

The orchestra would play the song in a Renaissance style, and the king would complain, "That's not right!" Then one by one, everyone came in and tried to make King Irving happy by playing it their way. These were third graders playing and acting, with a sixth grader as narrator. Throughout the musical numbers there were jugglers, and dancers crossing the stage, using every talent they had.

King Irving declares whichever girl can correctly play *Twinkle,*

Twinkle Little Star can marry his son, the Prince and famous dragon slayer.

Then enters the "Braggart" claiming his daughter can play the song, and she's also the most beautiful girl in the kingdom. "Bring her here," said the King. "If your daughter can play, she'll marry my son. If *NOT*, she'll be locked up in the tower for the rest of her life—and *you*, sir, will lose your head!"

"Oh, my goodness, what have I done?" the Braggart sings in a medley of songs. His beautiful daughter proves she can't read music, play piano or anything. So she's locked in the tower with a harpsichord and a blackboard with the melody of the song written on it.

With a week to learn the song and to play the instrument, through the window comes a hip musician named Rumpelstiltskin who promises to teach her to read the music and play the keyboard.

"*BUT* you will have to give me your first child!" he says. So she promises, having no choice, and at the end of the week she plays the song before the King perfectly and all the evil spells are broken. (End of Act One.)

Act Two is a year later. The Princess, now a mother, is in the garden with the baby, and Rumpelstiltskin demands the child. But his heart softens and he says, "If you guess my name, I'll go away,"

So the Princess sends off her ladies-in-waiting to all the night clubs in the Magic Kingdom to find out who this musician is—followed by kids playing music from the different places they went.

They finally spot him playing in one of the clubs, tell the Princess his name, and when he returns, she shouts out his name! (The End.)

We did this and dozens of other plays, while I had fun teaching music to each student in the school. Combining silliness with the study of serious music enabled them to learn and perform the words and music right from the start.

DR. WILLIAM E. DAHLBERG

DR. GUY HO

42 A Legend In His Time
by William E. Dahlberg, D.D.S.

"Even now, after thirty years, every time I work on a crown or a bridge, I can feel Dr. Ho looking over my shoulder."

This and similar statements are common among Dr. Guy C. Ho's former USC dental students. A Dental Hall of Fame honoree in 1986, Dr. Ho taught dental anatomy, among many other subjects, from 1940 to 1965. His demand for excellence and his lifelong impact on thousands of dental school graduates over the years are best illustrated by the story told by his daughter after she had been a guest at the San Diego Yacht Club.

When the commodore identified himself as a graduate of USC's dental school, she proudly suggested that he might know her father. "Do I know him?" he shouted. "When I was a freshman I hated him more than any man in the world." Seeing the shocked expression on her face and sensing her desire to crawl under the table, he quickly added, "But let me finish my story.

"When I was a sophomore I didn't think he was so bad, although he still made us work hard. But in the next year or two I learned to love him as a teacher. After we left school we really remembered him. Please tell him that any time he wishes to visit San Diego I would be honored to have him as my guest here at the Yacht Club."

Dr. Ho was born in China a decade after the 1912 revolution in the city of Nanking. He was one of six children born to a very prominent dentist in the region along the Yangtze River, 200 miles north of Shanghai. All of the top Chinese foreign merchants and government officials were his father's patients, including the president of China. Guy was practically born in the dental office that was in front of the 20-room mansion his father designed and built. In his early teens his father put him to work in his lab carving teeth, because of Guy's precocious skill with his hands.

Many of his father's patients lacked the currency to pay him, so they bartered for his service with collectibles such as rare and ornate weapons. When the Ho family fled the 1949 Communist takeover, many of these treasures, especially the guns, were considered too dangerous to try to take out of the country. The fear of being caught with weapons outweighed the loss of millions of dollars in today's market value for these rare treasures.

Guy's parents had met in Honolulu, Hawaii, where his father was beginning his practice. His mother was a "picture bride." His father saw the picture of his best friend's sister that was included in a letter from the friend's family who lived in Hongkong, and he loved the face that he saw. They were engaged by mail and he sent for her.

His new wife's father was a minister and her mother was a physician, so they had many worthwhile connections that could be very influencial in promoting a young dentist's career. In four years they'd had two baby girls and, because her family had always had servants, she was ill prepared for the rigorous challenges of being a wife, homemaker, mother, cook, etc. The thought of returning to a more comfortable lifestyle in China was very appealing to both of them. So they carefully saved the required $800 dollars and the little family returned to her homeland. This proved to be a wise decision because, in less than a month, Guy's father quickly made back the $800 dollar travel expense in his new practice.

Guy had to finish college at Nanking University in 1936 before he was permitted by the government to study abroad. During his last year, his sister, a graduate music student at USC was having dinner with University President Rufus von Kleinschmidt. She casually mentioned that her brother intended to come to America to study dentistry at an eastern college, telling the president of his extraordinary skills. The President arose, excused himself and immediately telephoned Dean Ford of the dental school, who sent a cablegram to China, accepting Guy sight unseen.

He arrived the third week in September, several weeks late for the start of the semester. Informed that his class was already filled, he told the registrar, "I didn't travel 7,000 miles to hear this!" However, someone conveniently dropped out at the last moment, and his dental career was underway. Within weeks after arriving, in spite of language difficulties, he had not only caught up, but with his 10 years of lab experience, was even tutoring classmates.

He met his wife Elsie when he attended a Chinese Students' Club meeting on the evening of his arrival in Los Angeles. She had come to USC from Hawaii as a scholarship student in the Department of Sociology and Social Welfare.

Upon graduation in 1940, Dean Ford offered him a teaching position. Intending to return to assume his father's practice, he instead remained on the USC faculty for 25 years. He taught in four different departments: dental materials, prosthetics, dental anatomy, and fixed prosthodontics, and became famous for his endless supply of jokes and his delight in telling them for comic relief during his lectures.

But Dr. Ho could strike fear into the hearts of freshman students with those two infamous words, "Do ovah!" He had the almost inhuman ability to pull out his pocket knife and carve a tooth out of wax to perfection—freehand! When challenged by a careless student who might have worked for hours on carving a similar model of questionable quality and shape, he would often do this in just a few minutes while they watched in fascination—and the measurements of *his* instant, jewel-like artwork were never off. No wonder the San Diego commodore remembered him well.

As famous as he was for his strictness, his sense of humor was equally legendary. He often said he loved outdoor Christmas decorations. Many of the festive homes he passed with their thousands of lights, Santa's sleigh and reindeer, also had his name in huge letters on their roofs— "HO, HO, HO."

BERNADENE HIGH COLEMAN

Bernadine High Coleman was born in rural Louisiana, and grew up in Los Angeles. She received her M.S. from Loyola-Marymount and her B.A. from California State University, Los Angeles. She attended UCLA School of Writing.

Mrs. Coleman is the author of two novels, *Mama Rose* and *I Leave You My Dreams* and a book of poetry, *Listen My Children*. She resides in Southern California.

43 **Letting Go**
by Bernadene High Coleman

When you have what you consider the happiest marital union on the face of the earth and then you suddenly lose that spouse, you enter a state of grief that is indescribable. My first reaction was shock and numbness, where I remained for several days. This period was followed by denial. There are times when you think there is no way to move beyond grief. For me, the pain was deep and I moved through a wide range of overwhelming emotions.

Fortunately, I have great friends and family who spent long hours just talking to me. We talked about my life from the beginning to the present. They reminded me of many of the blessings that filled my life, blessings that many of them had shared. Eventually, I was able to express some of my deepest and most intimate feelings, and the time came when the hurt was gradually replaced with moments of laughter and lighthearted banter. I felt lucky to be surrounded by people who loved me, people who were soon able to convince me that "life was worth living." Soon there were signs that a healing had begun.

We spoke of others who had gone through the same experience and had managed to overcome. But my grief was less manageable when I was left alone. By now I knew that individuals had varying degrees of grieving and of being left alone. For me, being left alone was the greatest obstacle of all. Everywhere I went I seemed to see couples talking, laughing and enjoying each other. It was difficult for me to accept that I did not have my life partner to do simple things like go to a restaurant, go to a movie or go for a walk in the park. He was not there to discuss a good book, the events of the day or family gossip.

A friend sent me an announcement from a Grief Counseling Workshop. Earlier, my doctor had suggested this activity, but somehow I never followed through. Now, in my loneliness, I decided to give it a try.

The workshop was just what I needed. It gave me new hope and courage to reinvest myself in the process of living and finding happiness. I began to cope with eating out and going to plays alone. I did it because often I had no choice.

Exactly one year after the death of my husband, I accepted an invitation to a party that I really had no interest in attending. My cousin, who was the host, always gave parties where the guests ended up playing cards and drinking lots of beer, neither of which I did. As I sat on the couch alone, an attractive man entered the room, said hello and introduced himself. He engaged me in a conversation that commanded my complete attention. He talked about the importance and the need for community volunteers to give not only their time but also their resources. Volunteering is an activity that is near and dear to my heart, as I have volunteered in my community for many years.

This tall, handsome and articulate man then brought up the subject of astrology. I had to admit that I knew very little about astrology, but that it had always fascinated me. After telling about my sign and its meaning, he offered me his business card and suggested that I call him.

I have to tell you that I was interested. Not only was he easy to look at, he was well-dressed, easy to talk to, and a good conversationalist, which is attractive to me. After clearing that protocol of *my calling him* with my son, I phoned the gentleman two days later.

"Perhaps you won't remember me, but I met you the other night at a party ..."

"Of course I remember; you're the lovely lady whose sign is Gemini. How could I forget such a charming woman? I was hoping you would call, and you did. You have made my day!" He interrupted before I completed my sentence.

"I am impressed. How are you?"

"I would be much better if I could see you again. Is that a possibility?" he asked.

Because he was a friend of my cousin's, I responded that I thought we could arrange that. "I walk every morning. How about meeting me at the track?" He knew the track.

"Just tell me when; I'll be there."

That week he met me early each morning; after we walked four laps around the track, it was time for him to leave. I finished the last two laps thinking how fortunate I was to meet someone of his caliber. An erudite, caring, single businessman. A man in my age bracket. A man I could easily relate to.

We talked on the phone each evening and he always asked me to call before retiring, just to say goodnight. One week later, he invited me out to an elegant restaurant for dinner. The meal and the conversation were phenomenal. So I agreed to begin a friendship with this incredible man who was interested in me. This man who made me feel alive again. I would sometimes pinch myself in order to know if I were dreaming this scenario. I was beginning to recognize that Todd was a man I could easily consider for a serious relationship. We were in the hand-holding stage, with light kisses to greet each other, and again to say good night. Nothing serious yet, but I felt that romance was on the horizon.

Todd was a man any woman would be proud to be seen with and would be delighted to introduce to her friends and family. He was always complimenting me, even making me laugh and go long periods of time without thinking of my loss. I knew that he was good for me.

During the next month, we went to a formal banquet, the theater and out to dinner on two occasions. He shared with me that his two children worked in the business with him. Both his son and daughter were married. Only the daughter had a child. I told him about my sons, but I knew it was not yet the time to introduce them, although I was anxious to do so.

One of the most important lessons I had learned in my workshop on grief was to give myself permission to release the grief. Also, you should give yourself permission to love again and to find joy in living. I was at the threshold of looking ahead.

The following Saturday, I received a call from Todd.

"How about brunch tomorrow, can you do it?"

"Yes, I can after church. What time will you pick me up?"

"Can you meet me at Barnaby's at two o'clock? I might be running late."

"See you there," I said.

I drove to the hotel whose restaurant happens to be one of my favorite places to dine. All the while I felt blithesome feelings that I had met someone who had given me just the lift I needed to get on with living. He had helped me put my loneliness and sadness somewhere on a back burner.

Todd was sitting in a lounge in the lobby when I entered. The smile on his face was captivating. A wonderful feeling of warmth flooded my entire body when I saw him. I was thankful that he had restored joy in my life. He greeted me with a kiss and a loving embrace.

"Thank you for meeting me," he said in a glad voice.

"The pleasure is mine."

We sat there for a while drinking Midoris. We were in the middle of brunch when he began to explain why he could not pick me up.

"Jasmine's grandmother went to church and I had to watch her until she returned to take over. I had a hunch she would not return in a timely fashion," he began.

"I don't think I understand." I stammered.

"My granddaughter, Jasmine, spent the weekend at the house and I had to wait for her grandmother to return before I could leave."

"Are you telling me that you have a wife?" Again I stammered, my body shaking.

"My wife still lives in our home."

"You never told me anything like that."

"You never asked. But I'll explain the circumstances."

The floor fell from under me and I did everything I possibly could to maintain some degree of poise. My equilibrium was deserting me and the room began to spin, and to top it all, I was trying hard to catch my breath, which was desperately fleeing my lungs. It wasn't the Midoris.

"Bernadene, please—don't make more out of this situation than there is. My ex-wife and I live in the same house. It is purely a business agreement. She is my second wife. When my first wife divorced me, we had to sell the business and the house and divide everything. It was the attorneys who ended up with the money we had worked so hard to accumulate. We ended up with nothing but a worthless marriage. I had to begin again from scratch. When I met Ellen, we made an agreement that if the marriage did not work, we would stay together for the sake of the business. She worked along beside me to make the business what it is today, successful and thriving. We pledged not to let anything destroy what we have worked so diligently for. She goes her way and I go mine. We live independently of each other's private lives. You've been calling me nightly. Did she ever answer my phone? I will answer for you. She has her own phone and I have mine. She dates others and so do I and we don't question or interfere with each other's privacy."

He noted the expression on my face and then added. "Bernadene, some people live like that. Have you been that secluded? We're not the only couple who have done this. I can name you some of the couples. I know you will be shocked since you didn't seem to know this was going on. You even know some of the couples that are living this exact same way, right now. I'll name some of them; two are your neighbors. John and Hazel . . ."

"Please don't." I pleaded. "I don't care what other couples do. If they are happy living that way, then I am happy for them; it's just not the life style I can handle."

"You and I have something great going, please don't walk away from it. I knew the moment I laid eyes on you, you were a special person; don't end it without giving careful consideration and thought to what the two of us could mean to each other. I love and adore you and I think you should give our being together a chance before you just walk out. I know we can work this out. We have so much in common."

"Todd, to continue to see you under the circumstances you explained could never work for me. I am a 'territorial' woman. I need to know that I am the sole proprietor of the territory. I could never share the man I love with another woman and I could never give myself to another woman's man, even though you tell me that it's okay. My heart says it isn't," I said. "My soul tells me it's not okay. But I owe you something. I will forever be grateful that you gave me back my life. You stirred feelings in me that I thought were buried with my husband. You let me know that I can love again and that I can share that love with someone who loves me. You gave me the capacity to hear music again, to laugh, to dance and to have joy. I love you, Todd, for all that and even beyond, but I could never love you in the way you need and deserve to be loved.

You are a beautiful man and I shall always cherish the brief time we had together and I shall never know what it might have been."

I gave a shocked Todd a big kiss and stood up to leave without finishing my meal. Before he could protest, I was out the door. My emotions were totally in check and I felt wonderful to have come through such an abrupt turn of events without frustration or sadness. In that moment, I knew I was the recipient of a priceless gift.

Two days later, as I walked around the track, Todd fell in step beside me.

"Is it okay if I walk with you?"

"Of course it is. You look great! Is that a new jogging suit?"

"I miss you." He said in a sad voice. "Won't you reconsider our friendship? You know we almost had a great thing going. I don't want to give up on us yet."

"Todd, you should have leveled with me from the beginning."

"Bernadene, you're the only one who has had a problem with understanding my situation."

"I am sorry, Todd. This is painful for me too, but I don't know any other way to handle it. Your situation goes against the grain of my way of living. I don't think I could ever accept it."

"You could at least give it a trial run; it isn't too late."

"I'll give it some thought," I lied.

I knew I could never expose myself to unknown elements of that kind of relationship. I was much too fragile to even consider the odds of such a venture. I was fortunate to have come to the point of giving myself permission to begin living again, and I would not take any chance of a reversal of my good fortune.

MARGARET HAYDEN RECTOR

44 The Evening Purse
by Margaret Hayden Rector

All my life, if I could not afford something, I would go *visit* it, instead.

If there was a dress I loved in the store and I couldn't afford it, I would go visit it until someone else purchased it. My coveted dresses never seemed to go on sale. They would just be purchased or be finally withdrawn and disappear somehow.

This was also true of jewelry. If it was too expensive, I simply went to visit it—until the same thing usually happened.

This personal approach of mine took over, when six years ago in Beverly Hills, I saw an evening purse in the Judith Leiber Shop at the Beverly Hilton Hotel.

I fell in love with the purse. It was art nouveau in style, in a white satin material, and trimmed with what I thought must be semi-precious moonstones. But most of all, it had a shoulder chain you couldn't help but love both in quality and the way it was engineered into the interior of the purse. Levers always had to be drawn down or up for it to be in correct position—for it to open or close properly.

The interior of the purse was also very special. There were three compartments. The center section contained a little satin change purse, a swivel mirror which could even sit on a table, and a little metal comb with a *silk* tassel attached. *All* of these items carried Judith Leiber's name.

I knew she was one of the world's great purse designers and manufacturers. Each month, with the exception of the summer period, I attended the Edna Davidson Book Salon at the Beverly Hilton, without exception on the third Tuesday of the month. It had been going on for thirty-six years. I myself had been a member for about half that long.

After the luncheon, authors' talks and autographing sessions, I would leave the Hilton by way of the main lobby and always stop to admire my purse. It was usually in the same location at a side display window.

For six years I did this unfailingly, always with the realization that it was way out of my price range.

Two months ago, I stopped by again. I stood still. My heart seemed to miss *more* that one beat. I could not find my purse. Because of Merv Griffin's remodeling, everything had been moved around. When the Judith Leiber Shop had been finally returned to its original location, everything in its display was relocated.

Where was my purse? Not in the window. Not in any glass case inside. Nowhere! The saleslady saw the dismayed look on my face and asked if she could help. I described the purse.

"Oh, that one?" she chortled. "It's over here. It's shopworn, dear. So it's half price."

I gasped. There it was—my purse. "Did you say shopworn?"
"Yes."
"Did you say half price?!!"
"Yes."
"It's mine!"

I proudly wrote out a check from my own personal checkbook.

She put the purse into a special Judith Leiber protective bag and handed it to me.

"I'm sorry it's shopworn, dear."

I shook her hand and moved to the door. "Don't be. Of course it's shopworn—you see, I've been *visiting* it for six years!"

DON ALBRECHT

Don Albrecht comes from a mining background. His family came to northern California during the gold rush and settled in the Manhattan Bar area of the American River. His great-great uncle, C.E.W. Albrecht, owned a prominent miners' general store east of Auburn known as the Grizzly Bear House. His grandfather Milton Monroe and father Donald Leo grew up there. Albrecht is a docent with the Placer County Museums Docent Guild (Past President), and with the California State Division of Mines and Geology.

45 **Gold Fever**
by Don Albrecht

California became the 31st state of the union on September 9, 1850, following two dramatic events: the first and well-known discovery of Gold at Sutter's Mill on January 24, 1848, in the area now called Coloma on the American River.

The second, not so well remembered, was when our government signed the Treaty of Guadalupe Hidalgo with Mexico on February 2, 1848, *only nine days later.*

Neither Mexico or the United States could have known about the gold strike, given the slow state of cross-country communications. For example, it took four days from the initial finding by a carpenter named James A. Marshall to let his employer, Captain John Sutter, know about it only 60 miles away.

At the time of their meeting on January 28, Sutter requested that it be kept secret for fear of panic and a land rush. He had just received a large land grant (nearly 50,000 acres) from the Mexican Governor of California and he needed time to develop this new area. So it was several weeks before the news of the gold discovery finally did leak out.

There was an important event which led to the wide-spread knowledge of gold being found. Highly qualified workers just released from the U.S. Army in September of 1847 were looking for work. They were members of the Mormon Battalion. After their cross-country trek from Ft. Leavenworth, Kansas to San Diego, California, 150 of them set out to return to their families, now in the territory of Utah, by the northern route through San Francisco, then called Yerba Buena. Half remained in northern California to find work, and Captain Sutter offered employment to about 40 of them to help develop all this new land. One of the necessary projects was the building of a flour mill downstream near Sutter's Fort, and a saw mill on the river to the east of it. James Marshall was assigned to supervise the construction.

About half of the newly hired men went with Marshall to first dig the "head and tail traces"— a ditch to carry water. When the digging was completed and the water was released, it flowed so swiftly it completely washed away the mill's rough foundation. Examining the damage, Marshall found yellow nuggets exposed in the wet soil. These were later assayed as gold with each piece worth as much as $5 (100 times more if it were to be assayed today). After Marshall left for Sutter's Fort, the mill workers continued looking for gold. At first the few outsiders who heard about it didn't believe it, even when Marshall's men showed them the evidence.

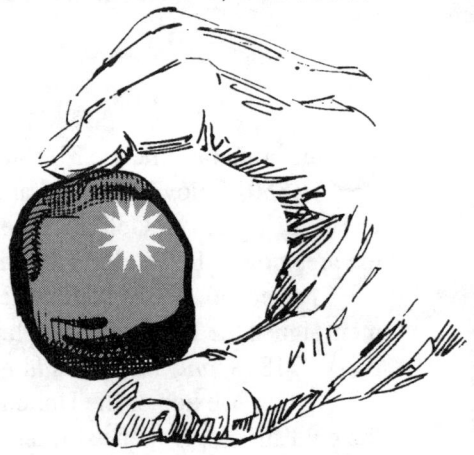

Sam Brannan, a Sutter's Fort store owner and a shrewd businessman from Yerba Buena, immediately visited the discovery site, finding out for himself about the gold. He obtained enough gold to fill a small bottle and returned to rent the largest house Sutter owned and converted it into a large merchantile store, ready to sell supplies to future gold miners. He shipped in everything he could find that might be useful for gold mining via flatboat up the Sacramento River to his store. Then, on May 15, 1848, he went to Portsmouth Square in downtown San Francisco and held up the bottle shouting "*Gold! GOLD! **G-O-L-D!***—from the American River!" Everybody within sound of his voice went wild with gold fever.

The local citizenry closed their stores and left their houses half built; sailors abandoned ships in the harbor, soldiers deserted their posts at the Presidio, and everyone headed for the gold fields. The wave of excitement rolled on to San Jose, the capitol city of Monterey, and south to Los Angeles. Sam Brannan, who started it all, had positioned himself to make a fortune. From there the word spread, was soon grossly exaggerated, and eventually caused an influx of gold seekers from all around the world.

Gold was again discovered in quantity in a place later known as Auburn Ravine, east of what is now the city of Sacramento, on May 16, 1848, by a Frenchman named Claude Chana. He was a worker on Sicard's Ranch on the Bear River and he heard the many stories of gold. So he set out with a party of Indian workers to explore for himself and on the first night out they camped near a stream. Chana dipped a pan in the gravel and immediately found several sizable pieces of gold.

Auburn became the historical center of the gold rush with its vast amounts of easily found gold. Over 90% of all the gold *ever* found in the world has dated from 1848. News of rich "clean-ups" ($500 a pan, $15,000 from five carloads of "dirt" at $12 per ounce) brought huge numbers of '49ers to the Placer County area.

This was followed by gold discoveries on the Yuba River at Rich Flat, and was soon to be found in paying quantities virtually *everywhere* throughout a large area. All of these valuable findings soon labeled the area as the "North Fork Dry Diggings."

The Guadalupe Hidalgo Treaty gave the United States the vast area from Utah to California for only $15 million dollars. Within a few weeks of the signing, this "gold fever" struck California and busy mining camps sprung up as other major strikes were made.

All this proved to the government in Washington, D.C. the potential wealth of the large gold fields in California. It was the focus of President Polk's message to Congress on December 8, 1848. This officially started the worldwide gold rush of 1849.

Because of gold fever, California's 1848 population of only 26,000 exploded to 380,000 by 1860, growing by almost 15 times in only 12 years. The discovery of gold preceded future discoveries of oil, the development of the agricultural wealth of the central valleys, and the eventual industrial bonanzas of motion pictures, aerospace and computer technology.

So, from the sprawling ranchos and missions—a lazy land rich in climate but poor in resources—California has grown to become the seventh largest economy in the world, all of which started by accident on that fateful day in 1848.

SUSAN MOSS

46 Cancer Saved My Life
by Susan Moss

How is it that a frightening, "terminal" disease could turn into one of the greatest opportunities of my life? A terrifyingly horrible diagnosis turned out to be a tremendous resource for my own life, and now that of others, worldwide.

That cold, overcast day in December of 1990, I had gone to my gynecologist, Dr. Wayne C. Furr, (a good name for a gynecologist), for a check up. I hadn't felt ill at all. It was just my regular, once-a-year visit to make sure nothing was wrong.

But something was wrong. Very wrong. Dr. Furr found a tumor in my left breast. He touched it, pulling his hand back with a start, as if he had touched a hot stove. He turned white. He put my hand on the rock in my breast. He already knew the diagnosis. I had breast cancer.

He completed the exam, only to find in further shock that I also had a tumor in my uterus. Again, he knew the diagnosis. I also had uterine cancer.

"See a surgeon!" he ordered me.

I was stunned. Didn't cancer make you sick? I did not feel ill. Maybe he was wrong. I knew he was an experienced and highly-regarded gynecologist, however. I knew he knew.

"I'll get a mammogram," I volunteered, trying to stave off the cutting-up of my body parts, trying to buy time.

He acted as if it didn't matter. He already was certain. There is such a thing as touch-diagnosis. An experienced doctor can tell what a tumor is by feeling it. A rock-hard tumor like mine almost always signifies cancer. Nevertheless, he consented to my delaying tactics. I knew that mammograms were highly inaccurate, especially in dense breasts like mine. I knew X-rays were dangerous.

My friend Kimberly had had a mammogram for her breast tumor that she found herself. It had come out negative. Yet a subsequent biopsy revealed she had cancer.

I had watched her go through a harrowing, destructive medical treatment. They had amputated her beautiful, full breast. She had then vomited her way through chemotherapy and sustained two broken ribs from excessive radiation. For all her sacrifice, this torture was not working to stop the cancer from growing. It had returned in exactly the same spot! It had grown back in the chest wall where her breast used to be! She was now fighting for her life as the cancer metastasized into her lungs. Later it would go into her brain, intestines, and other parts of her body. She was only thirty-four when she had found the lump. She was to die at age thirty-eight, one week after her birthday, without hair, emaciated and in terrible pain.

My mammogram was negative. "That means I'm off the hook, doesn't it?" I asked Dr. Furr. He shook his head. He began to call me every day at the studio demanding in sharp, loud terms that I see a surgeon.

"No!" I stated over and over. He seemed never to get the message. Finally, he gave in. "Come back in two months," he instructed.

To this, I agreed. I made the appointment with his nurse.

I decided to create my own health program I called MOTEP, Marathon Olympic Tumor Eradication and Prevention program. This program would cover every aspect of my life: physical, mental, spiritual, emotional, diet, exercise, visualization, group therapy, and topical natural treatments. Laughter, love, establishing the feeling of peace within myself with chanting and prayer, were also crucial.

The body works with a deadline. Just as if you must stop a certain number of feet to obey a red light, or have a certain amount of time to write a paper, a deadline is a fact the body and mind understand. If you can coordinate your vision, muscles, nerves, bones—not to mention your car, to stop at the red light, then perhaps the coordination of the immune system with enough support from your health-oriented efforts could also meet a deadline. It didn't seem like magic at the time to me. I believed I could do it, refusing to give in to my fright. I refused to consider what I would do if it didn't work.

If I die, I die, I decided. But I'm going to give this my best effort. It seemed to me that cancer was a degenerative disease. To overcome cancer it was necessary to regenerate—in other words, to get into shape, detoxify, and de-stress the body and bring the general health back up to a superior state. I knew I had been under tremendous stress in the past year-and-a-half. The art market, so strong in the '80s, had all but disappeared in 1989. I was struggling financially. A man with whom I thought I was in love talked constantly about his other girl friends and ex-wife. He finally went off to marry one he had dated off-and-on for twenty years. I was devastated.

I knew that I had my work cut out for me. Financial problems, jealousy and depression had eroded my health completely. I was tense, angry, isolated and saturated with self-pity. Even my exercise program had degenerated into sitting in a hot tub at the gym feeling sorry for myself, instead of my usual hour of high-impact aerobics and swimming laps. I had lost my enthusiasm for life.

I spent the next two months detoxifying my body and destressing my mind. I joined the YMCA and swam a mile every morning. While swimming, I visualized a scud missile hitting my tumor, seeing the white particles being blown into smithereens in the water ahead of me. In the sauna, I visualized my tumor as butter and melting. I detoxified my body with fresh carrot juice, orange juice, and whole grains like barley and brown rice, and lots of vegetables and fruits. I eliminated meat and dairy products from my diet and under-ate for a month. This allowed my body to throw out lots of junk. I had accumulated toxins and excess meat and fats I couldn't digest that had backed up in my colon.

Once cleaned and detoxified, fortified with group therapy, prayer, and strong visualization so that I would be able to meet my deadline, my body went into a shocking healing reaction. My breast turned bright neon red, hot to the touch and hard as stone. My left arm became gigantic, swelled and paralyzed, reminding me of a freeway pillar.

I was shocked. But instead of calling 911, I continued on my program, swimming with one arm. That lasted only about a day-

and-a-half. A week later, doing the breast exam in the sauna, I was amazed to find that my tumor had disappeared! Not only that, the tumor in my uterus that was getting so big it was pressing on my back and giving me back pains, had also apparently gone. I had no pain!

Dr. Furr, at my appointment, was incredulous. He could not believe I had no tumors and kept up the exam in a most perplexed manner, going from one breast to the other. He literally jumped on them, trying with all his might to find any tumor. "It was right there!" he stated, confused.

Yes, it *was* right there.

He finally gave up. "What did you do?" he asked.

"I went swimming," I said laughing.

Dr. Furr encouraged me to do a video. I decided to write a book first. *Keep Your Breasts! Preventing Breast Cancer the Natural Way* is now in its sixth printing and in every Barnes and Noble bookstore in the country. In 1999, I got a two-week trip, all expenses paid, to Europe when the book was translated and came out in Germany and Holland. In Germany, the book is now in its fourth printing. I had a wonderful visit in Berlin and saw the apartment house where my mother was born.

I also learned a great lesson. How to take care of myself, and to let anger, frustration, jealousy and other negative feelings go. To not let negative feelings eat away at my body, internalizing my frustrations, but to be able to forgive, to help others, and to laugh at myself and my foibles. Most of all I learned never to get "stuck" again. There is always a way out of problems, and that way is to turn them into the tremendous opportunities like those I have received as a health-book author.

Not only did I have another way to earn my livelihood, I had a mission. I had a way to help people save their own life, and to understand the mystery of cancer, which is no mystery at all. There are definite causes that one must face and change to overcome disease. The will to live must be bolstered. Appreciation of life must be renewed. A health program must be initiated. You can save your own life. Life is precious.

Most of all, I had a new way to look at the world. Gone was the self-centered person who was often rude to others because, after all, I was this "Great Artist." I had really used cancer as a self-growth opportunity, a way of reviewing my life and seeing that my ego and one-sided direction were making me ill.

I began to be a kinder person. I began to see that Karma really worked. Helping others resulted in amazing rewards I had never sought. My life became so much richer. And I even got my first limousine ride!

Cancer had saved my life.

SOL H. MARSHALL

Sol H. Marshall states that he has held only one "real job" in his life—typing addressograph plates for one week. Otherwise, he has enjoyed being a social worker, newspaper editor and publicity director. Telephone him at (818) 893-3565 for stories on his interesting life from coast to coast.

47 **The Keys to My Success**
by Sol H. Marshall

Typing—two fingered—saved my life when I joined the Army during World War II.

It was all accidental because I once was asked to help the sports editor of the college paper. Later I became the sports editor, and then editor of the paper.

I was drafted in 1941 at New York, then bussed to Fort Dix, New Jersey, where we received our uniforms and equipment. We sat, talked, drilled, marched, hiked and were constantly exhausted. The sergeants kept us busy.

What a future, I thought. "How can I get out of this?" So I went into the company office and found the sergeant who was mumbling over a stack of papers. I walked up to his desk, leaned over and said, "What kind of typewriter is that? Kind of looks like mine."

He jumped up, and said, "You know how to type?"

"I sure do," I said.

"Come here and sit down," he said. Some notes were lying on the desk, and he pointed to a form titled "Morning Report."

He said, "See what yesterday's Report looks like. Take these notes and enter them on today's Report here, in the same way."

So I did.

He said, "Just hang around here, in case I have to type anything else. There's coffee, so help yourself."

I sat around until Mess Call for dinner. He said, "Listen. When they line you up after breakfast tomorrow, tell them you're supposed to report to me."

So I did.

I spent the three days at Fort Dix in the office. My fellow recruits spent their time learning to march, drill, handle rifles, listening to endless lectures, then more marching, marching, marching, hiking, hiking, hiking.

Later all of us were sent to Camp Lee, Virginia, the location of Quartermaster School. Class schedule was 9 a.m. to noon; then 1 to 3 p.m. and included training for cooks, supply people, truck drivers, among other specialties. Again I went into the company office and volunteered to the sergeant with the most stripes on his sleeve. I leaned over his shoulder saying, "How's that typewriter working?"

He looked up at me and said, "If I knew, I could get this Report done a lot easier."

I said, "I know how to type. Let me try it." So I did.

He said, "Listen, when you get through with your classes tomorrow, you come in here. If they ever want to take you out to drill, march, or anything else, tell them you're supposed to report to the office for a special assignment. Then come here."

I learned how a headquarters office operates, which was the same for every echelon up the line. I did NOT have to learn about KP duty (Kitchen Police, meaning washing dishes, pots and pans) or walking guard duty at night.

We graduated in 90 days, and were sent to Camp Shenango in Pennsylvania, a kickoff point for overseas duty. The first day I spotted the first sergeant in Company A and made the same approach as before. "How are you fixed for office help? I can type, and I ran the headquarters office at Camp Lee."

"Hey, I can use you." Sgt. Smith said. "What's your name again?"

As before, everything was running well in a short time. Just before noon one Friday, Sgt. Smith said, "I'm taking off for a few days. I'll see you Monday."

And he was gone!

Monday, before noon, the first lieutenant came to tell me Sgt. Smith caught chicken pox over the weekend. "Can you take care of things?" he asked.

With a single stripe on my sleeve, I was Acting First Sergeant with a company of 687 enlisted men and 17 officers on my hands.

My management and typing skills improved as we prepared to ship out to the European Theater.

I landed in England exactly one year from the day I joined the

Army in New York. Same routine—"I know how to type," I said to the first company clerk I met. Soon after being assigned and equipped with a typewriter, I looked out the window as the rest of my company, all 423 of them, marched out with carbines slung over their shoulders. D-Day was only a few days away.

Several weeks later, I was permanently assigned to London, with my papers marked "KTP—Key Type Personnel" as a staff sergeant.

Almost two years later, the invasion of Europe behind us and the war nearly over, I saw a sergeant who had been in Company A. He told me our group had landed at Omaha Beach the day after D-Day. "We jumped off when our landing craft hit shallow water. We filled in for men who had died the first day. Most of us were trained as cooks or supply personnel, but we were told to 'Drive those trucks!'

"The enemy had been ready for the invasion. Their number one targets were the truck drivers."

I asked him, "How many are still around of the original 423?"

"Maybe a hundred of us," he said.

To this day the key to my success in community service remains that magic keyboard. My desire to volunteer has always served me well. Sixty years ago the typewriter absolutely saved my life.

VICTORIA BULLIS

Victoria Bullis is a professional psychic, life coach, and feng shui practitioner with over 30 years' experience. She is rated one of the top radio psychics in the country and has been on-air over 9,000 times in eight countries during the past 13 years. She has been featured in several books, as well as such magazines as *Harper's Bazaar* and *Harper's and Queen's* (England); and also writes self-improvement magazine articles.

Victoria, an interior designer, found herself living in Asia, which led to her studying feng shui. The study of numerous other metaphysical disciplines grew from there. She can be contacted at (888) 686-2200. Her website is www.victoriabullis.com.

48 **Hong Kong Blues**
by Victoria Bullis

When I first learned that my husband was being transferred to Hong Kong by the American chemical company he was working for, I was devastated. In my early 20s and newly married, I had just finished interior design school and was feeling that my life was as perfect as it could get. I had accepted an offer to work with a prestigious San Francisco design firm and was excited to begin; I was making friends in San Francisco society and was planning to join the Junior League.

Neither of us knew much about Asia. We had to look at a map to see where Hong Kong actually was. It sounded so foreign to me; I immediately began to conjure up notions about how miserable the way and quality of life in Hong Kong would be. I figured my life was over.

I organized the move, we said emotional goodbyes to all our many friends, and moved. It didn't take us long to find an apartment. Richard was adamant that he wanted to live in Stanley, a remote village on a bay a long way from where anything interesting was happening, such as shopping, restaurants, or offices. He said he wanted to be able to get away from the noise, pollution, and overcrowding of the frenetic business district, which was close to where most Americans lived. Stanley was the only bit of suburbia on Hong Kong Island. Even though I dreaded living at least an hour from anything that seemed at all western, with a heavy heart I gave in. Each time we'd come by taxi over the long, winding road from the sophisticated financial district hotel we'd been staying in, to look at possible places to live, I got car sick. The intense heat, exhaust fumes and twists in the road made me nauseated.

Our three bedroom apartment was one of six in an ugly concrete building perched on a bluff overlooking the South China Sea. Stanley was unique in the intensely populated, 50-plus story highrise apartment and office buildings in the then Colony of Hong Kong; it was a small fishing village comprised almost exclusively of Chinese and British inhabitants. The Chinese were either the few billionaires living in elegant compounds with dozens of guard dogs, or the fishermen (called 'boat people') living in junks in the harbor below our apartment building. The English were a combination of aristocrats and British Army families. None of the wives from either group worked, and their days centered around children, nannies, having tea, complaining and a rigid, closed social calendar. No one was at all interested in getting to know the one American now living there. And I *did* try so hard to break the ice.

My husband was traveling most of the time, selling agricultural chemicals to remote parts of Thailand, Indonesia, and the Philippines, and was exhausted or sick when he was home. Hong Kong was swelteringly hot and humid, and electricity was extremely expensive. So we allowed ourselves to use just one air conditioner, which we turned on only at night. We had purchased an ancient red MG that broke down constantly during the ride over Victoria Peak to the part of the island where most of the Americans and other foreigners lived. I *dreaded* driving it. I felt lonely, isolated, and miserable. On top of that, I didn't realize that I'd contracted a nasty parasitic infection that sapped all my energy; it was exhausting walking up the forty steps to my front door, so I stayed home a lot.

When I began to feel better, I knew that I needed to get out and do something to fill my lonely days, so I decided to throw myself into getting an interior design career going. This was a scary prospect, as I had no professional experience, and would be working in a city where the key people I needed to interact with on a daily basis didn't speak English. Not having anyone to network with, I tried advertising in a little shopping publication aimed at westerners, *The Dollarsaver*. After several weeks, I began to get some small—really small—jobs, such as window treatments, or slipcovers. I relished these contracts as they gave me something to do; I threw myself into each one.

Several months later, we began joining a few social clubs, and were on waiting lists for others. Business in Hong Kong was often conducted at one's clubs; thus they were a vital part of expatriate life. Through those, I finally started meeting a few new people, although, as with my neighbors, the women rotated their lives around playdates for their children, teas, and social obligations; only a handfull of these were Americans. Not having children, I found it took enormous effort on my part to fit in at all with them, even to get together for a lunch out somewhere. It was *very* slow going.

Having done volunteer work since I was 12, I figured from my past experience that I could make more contacts through volunteering. I called a few charitable organizations I'd read about in the local paper, such as Ox-Fam (an international relief organization), and signed up for numerous committees. Being an American was a disadvantage here, also, and I was given a lot of envelope-stuffing type of assignments.

Little by little, things finally started to improve, but I still felt lonely and an outsider. Eighteen months or so after arriving in Hong Kong, I saw an article in the *South China Morning Post* about a group of American women who were starting a local chapter of the League of Women Voters, a many-decades-old American institution. I "felt" something, got excited, and immediately tracked down the woman who'd been interviewed. She herself answered the phone, and signed me up for their introductory meeting the following week. I was barely able to wait for it to happen. Really hoping that I would finally be able to meet some new friends, I was ready to volunteer for whatever task forces or committees the league needed.

I arrived right on time at the "Mid-levels" address (the chic area I'd wanted to live in; high-rises full of Europeans and Americans) given to me. Afraid the MG might break down again, I'd taken a taxi all the way from Stanley. I rang the bell, the door opened, and there in front of me was Janet Auchincloss, Jacqueline Kennedy's half-sister. I was *floored*; I recognized her from having seen photos of her in *Town and Country* and other magazines. She was warm, welcoming, and ushered me in. She introduced me to the few women who had already arrived. Her home was a spacious, elegant, and stunningly beautiful apartment with views of Hong Kong harbor. The five or six other women seated in her living room were also open, gracious, and friendly. I became instantly overwhelmed. This was the happiest moment I'd experienced since arriving in the British Colony. I had goosebumps all over, and a strong feeling of anticipation that this would be the opening, or beginning, of the life I'd struggled to have for so long.

By the time I left, I had the phone numbers of several new League members. Some of the charities the group sponsored I knew I could sink my teeth into, and for the first time since my arrival in Hong Kong, I felt hope. When I excitedly relayed the day's events to my husband, telling him how thrilled I was to have met Janet, he replied, "Oh, I've been meaning to tell you, I'm going to be active on a committee recently started by several American businessmen. One of them is Lou Rutherford, Janet's husband. We met recently for lunch, and he proposed that the four of us get together for dinner one evening soon." While totally annoyed that he'd forgotten to tell me something that important, I was elated to be able to further my connection with Janet.

It took a couple of months before we had that dinner, but not for me to become involved with a group of women with whom I finally felt I had some connection. I attended most of the committee meetings, determined to be as much a part of my new-found social circle as possible. I began to be invited to luncheons, a lecture here or there on Asian art, and, occasionally, a weekend boating event. About six or so months later, one of my new friends asked if I'd like to volunteer at a Sotheby's Asian Antique auction coming to Hong Kong shortly thereafter. As now an avid collector of antique Chinese ceramics and pottery, I knew this was right up my alley, and I thrived on the involvement, which ended up becoming annual.

Richard began doing more and more with Lou to bring U.S. businesses to Hong Kong; he eventually became head of the American Chamber of Commerce there. I got to know Janet well through our husbands, League activities, and getting together often as friends. I made sure she knew I was there because I really liked her, and not because of her family or position in society. Feeling that, she allowed me to become a close friend. About the same time my circle of contacts began to grow and expand, my local British neighbors finally decided I was socially acceptable, and they started including me in their dinners, luncheons, boating events, and so on. From then on, both my personal and professional life took off, and I began to be known around town, both for interior design and by being seen at events. My picture occasionally was on the social pages of the two English language newspapers, and in the local English *Tatler*. I loved my life, and never wanted it to end.

I was active in numerous organizations, had a successful design business, learned and practiced feng shui, and reveled in traveling throughout the region. I collected Asian antiques, and even had a little line of semi-precious-stone jewelry in Bloomingdale's in New York, and lamps made from antique objects in a store in San Francisco. I became popular at dinners and was often invited despite Richard's frequent business travel. I particularly enjoyed working for and attending charity balls, a constant throughout the fall and winter. I now felt totally at home living in Stanley.

After some seven years in Hong Kong, Richard decided that he wanted to return to California. To no avail I begged him to change his mind. Since I had been brought up to believe I'd be married for life, it never occurred to me to remain there without him. My constant pleading wouldn't sway him, so I finally acquiesced and we moved back to San Francisco. Before leaving, I had vivid dreams and overwhelming intuition that I should stay there, and that everything would be all right. I cried daily as we went to our numerous farewell parties. I knew with every fiber of my being that I shouldn't go. But I did...

My father died soon after we moved into our new condo. Shortly after that, Richard met someone in his new office and asked me for a divorce. I still had trunks full of glamorous clothes, and no use for them, so I took them a dozen at a time to a resale shop. I was out of sync with friends I'd known before; now there were too many differences in our lifestyles. I slowly set up a design business, really hating to start the process of finding new clientele all over again.

Miserable in the city I was in, totally wishing to be back in the city and lifestyle I'd left, I tried to move back to Hong Kong. Staying there would have been one thing, but packing up from the west coast and moving back to one of the most expensive cities in the world was another. We'd had incredibly inexpensive rent which I couldn't get back again. For three years I actively tried to make it happen.

Two things kept me going. One was the knowledge that I'd get through this. I had done it before, survived it then, and would again. The second was my deep understanding of feng shui. From having practiced this ancient Chinese "Art of Placement" for several years, I this time had a fundamental belief that everything is temporary, and can easily be altered. I worked with every ritual and 'remedy' I knew, and things did turn around for me much more quickly than even I had anticipated.

Little by little, I began to think about practicing feng shui in the U.S. I knew from my own experience that it would help people transform their lives much faster and more easily than with the usual American modes of change. I had been taking classes in numerous related disciplines and became an avid student of everything metaphysical, from quantum mechanics to hypnotherapy. After a few people asked me to share with them how I "got" my information, regarding the placement of furniture in their homes, I

喜

HAPPINESS

decided to teach small workshops on design and feng shui. One thing led to another, and this has become my primary business; I do this on the radio, in groups, and with individuals. I get more joy out of doing this than I ever did with interior design; I truly love watching people shift their lives quickly, and often effortlessly.

I go back to Hong Kong a few times a year, often teaching classes as well as being a guest on an English language radio station. My hope has shifted to having a second home there one day; I am at ease there, and feel a part of it still in spite of all the changes in government. I continue to be a part of the social scene I loved so much when I lived there, although the number of people I used to know well has dwindled to only several.

I've since had to face other obstacles in life, but what I've learned is that no matter how far down you go, you *can* rise back up, and that it doesn't *have* to take the long time it did me when I crossed the globe to live in a strange land. Now, whenever I find myself with a difficult situation to deal with, I remind myself that I successfully turned around an untenable situation, and now have made the results my life's work.

HEALTH

DR. DEVRA Z. HILL

49 **Wild, Wild West!**
by Devra Z. Hill, Ph.D.

When one of my twin daughters, Shari, was only 12 years old, she became fascinated with the Mae West movies she saw on television. She found Mae to be not only entertaining and clever but also a very underestimated comedienne. She told me she wanted to meet Mae to interview her for the school paper, of which she was the editor. At that time, Mae West was alive and well and in her 80s.

Most kids who make a request like that would have little hope of accomplishing their desire, but in Shari's case, there was a distinct possibility it could be done. Her father, Irwin Zucker, a Hollywood publicity agent, had the connections to most of the stars in town and arranged the Mae meeting for Shari.

So it came to be that her request was granted by this legendary actress, but Mae made a request also. There were to be no cameras, no tape recorders and Shari would only be granted 15 minutes for her interview. Shari could take the old reliable pen and notebook and her old reliable mother to drive her to Mae's penthouse in the apartment building that Mae owned in Hollywood on Rossmore Avenue.

Well, it turned out to be quite an experience. For starters, Mae and Shari hit it off like old friends. Mae made her grand entrance about five minutes after her butler let us in.

In true Mae West elegance, she glided into the room on white high heeled pumps supporting her dainty feet and her white feather-trimmed floor-length satin gown. She still had her long, platinum-colored hair and was in full make-up. She wasn't about to let a fan see her au naturel, the way so many stars do these days.

In person, Mae was not a big woman, possibly five feet one,

but her ample bosom gave her the appearance of being much bigger when she graced the silver screen.

Everything in Mae's apartment was like a backdrop for her. White walls, white satin sofa, white satin-finished piano, and even her butler was dressed in white. It was easy to see what her favorite color was.

Mae told Shari stories about making movies in Hollywood's heyday, and how much she disliked W. C. Fields because he had abandoned his wife and children. It was Mae who was kind enough to send them money because W. C.'s imbibing of alcohol seemed to leave him without a conscience or a memory of his family. You could get an idea of his curmudgeon personality by one of his famous quotes: "Start the day out with a smile and get it over with!"

The designated 15 minutes stretched to three hours with Mae bringing out her scrapbooks depicting her career from the 1920s to the present 1970s, and telling my daughter that she was 28, and if you turn that around, you'd know how old she was! She said a reporter once called her a "gold digger," but she stated, "No gold digging for me, I take diamonds!" Something my daughter took to heart.

After three hours it was I, the weary mother, who said we had to leave. Then Mae graciously brought out some souvenir gifts for my delighted daughter: a silver bracelet, matching silver belt, and three autographed pictures of Mae. One for Shari's twin, Judi, one for me, and of course, one for Shari.

We were standing in Mae's doorway saying goodbye and thanking her for such an interesting afternoon when an earthquake hit and the whole building began to sway. Up to that moment Mae had spoken normally, but in a split second she went into her "Mae West" act, put her hand on her hip and in her famous on-screen sarcastic wit she said, "Well, you don't make much of an entrance, but you make one HELL of an exit!"

Of course, she broke the nervous tension and we all laughed through the next 20 seconds of shaking, proving that even at 82 she was still sharp and funny as ever. Also proving that one of her many famous quotes was also true about her, "It isn't what I do, but how I do it. It isn't what I say, but how I say it—and how I look when I do it and say it!"

We are glad we took to heart another famous quote of hers and went up to see her sometime. That "sometime" will stay in our memories forever.

Mae believed in the spirit world, telling us she had seen one of her dead relatives sitting on her sofa the week before.

Mae was born on August 17, 1893, and returned to the spirit world November 22, 1980, at the age of 87. We are sure she's got those spirits laughing in the great beyond right now!

Devra Z. Hill, Ph.D., has worn many hats. Currently, she's the author of *The Best of Your Life*, and previously scored success with a health book *Rejuvenate* and a novel *Three to Make Merry*.

She is also an entertainment reporter, voicing opinions on current movies for several radio stations across the U.S. with her "Hill" rating system—from the bottom to the top. They can be read on her web site: devrazhill.com and also for *In Magazine* inmag.com, then click on entertainment.

Married to Hollywood publicist Irwin Zucker for over 45 years, she is a doting grandmother to five grandchildren. She divides her time between homes in Beverly Hills and Santa Barbara, Calif., where all the kids live.

DR. AUDREY REED

Dr. Audrey Reed, author of *Money Toolbox for Women* and *Verbal Magik*, has 30 years experience in corporate and entrepreneurial sales, marketing and management. Dr. Reed's foundation of personal and financial mastery translates complex methodologies into simple, powerful practices, which she shares as a successful educator, lecturer and business coach. Dr. Reed is a NLP Master Trainer, has a B.A. in Business and a Doctorial Degree in Spiritual Science. **www.draudreyreed.com.**

50 Snapshots
by Audrey Reed, D.S.S.

I was sitting at my mother's bedside while she was in transition (she died Feb. 4, 2003). She was alert to all that was going on in her room. Snow was falling outside of her window. The room was warm and smelled of roses. We had been talking and Stuart, my husband, came into the room with a handful of old pictures. He was asking questions about my childhood, and I began to tell the bitterly funny "Mom Stories."

I understood at that moment that I might not have been as clear in my relationship with my mother as I thought.

I really wanted to be complete with any of the parent-child "stuff of life." We all have "stuff of life" with our parents, just because they are our parents.

I saw that there were snapshots of moments in my past that had not been cleared. I mean the "Mom Stories," like the tragedy of having secondhand tap shoes for my first tap class.

I felt anxious, time was ticking. It created a sense of urgency to discover the lesson and the blessing in each "Mom Story!" I wanted to find the gratitude contained in these stories, to further deepen the loving in our relationship.

* * *

I am four years old. We had walked blocks to get to the dance studio to register for tap lessons. While my mother registered me for the beginners' class, I was sitting on a bench ready to try on *the new shiny tap shoes*. I had been playing with a sample pair, expecting to take home new patent leather shoes, with a ribbed black ribbon and bright shiny new taps on the bottom. The taps would click— clack—snap when I hit the bottom of the shoe against the bench.

My mother came over to me with a beautiful pink box. I was excited! I opened it up and rustled through the white tissue paper. Inside were shoes that were slightly scuffed, and taps that didn't quite click—clack—snap the way new ones did. I was *angry!*

I believed that the kids would make fun of old scuffed shoes.

I flew into a tantrum!

My mother was embarrassed that I was throwing a tantrum in the studio, and hurt that I didn't appreciate the shoes. There was no hugging or cooing to calm me down, only a disappointed look on her face and a quick exit through the door.

That story got stuck in my four-year-old body and mind.

* * *

I adjusted my wonderfully inventive "camera" to *retake* the negative picture embedded in my memory. I put on my "wise woman" lenses. They contain all the lessons I have learned from the time I was four years old until now. My wise woman steps into the picture and stands by my four-year-old. My wise woman self reaches out to my four-year-old and hugs her tightly. My wise-woman self says, "You are very lucky to be taking lessons and look at these great shoes."

My four-year-old sees through my wise woman eyes that this is an extraordinary gift and a smart purchase. Look at the great ribbon ties the studio has put in the tap shoes and the shoes are in fabulously shiny condition. I can feel the ribbing in my hand. I can smell the shine polished on the shoes, and see the taps as they bounce back and forth. My mother has chosen the best. They will serve me well for the next few months, until I outgrow them. What a treasure! And I am going to be at dance class two days a week instead of one. **Snap!** A new picture—attach the new feeling, attune to the new lesson, realize the great blessing.

What I discovered is that Lenora Gross Fenning was a great mom. She always wanted me to have what I aspired to, in this case, dance lessons. She walked me to class twice a week, watched me practice and made sure the shoes she purchased at the dance studio, from the second hand "step up" program, were always the best ones in my size.

It was important to her that I took the lessons because it was very serious business for me at four years old.

I am extremely grateful she even took me back to the studio after the embarrassment and shock of my tantrum behavior.

* * *

This story's been a snapshot in my life photo album for years. This snapshot was fortified whenever we engaged the family life photo album of "Mom Stories." Now it's a new snapshot filled with love.

As a result, the "Mom Stories" have dissolved into love stories. The place that held them deep inside of me at the cellular level has been healed.

The lesson I learned from my wise woman place—my mother was tenacious and discerning. My mother wanted me to have the dance lessons. The lessons were a stretch for the family budget and she knew I would outgrow the shoes in months. I saw in a flash from my wise woman place that second-hand shoes were the best, the most loving solution.

By her bedside, with my head on her pillow, I whispered in her ear my thanks for her gifts of the shoes, the lessons, and mostly her devoted love.

For the next several hours, I sat with my mother and whispered thank you and gratitude for each of the Mom Stories I could remember that had shaped my life. Each negative story had been a rock or a sore point. I had carried my rocks in "Mom Stories" from childhood until now. I never realized how they closed off my heart. My mother smiled and nodded. Joyful healing tears slipped from her eyes as each old snapshot dissolved into a glorious gift, a lesson and a blessing.

I am richer for this process, grateful that it allowed me to complete this earth-time relationship with my mother in divine loving.

We always live with choice. She has taught me well how to influence the harmonic attunement towards a rich and balanced life. In adoration and appreciation of her soul's journey home— she is blessed.

PATRICIA RUST

Patricia Rust was a child model, best known as "The Ivory Soap Girl," which helped pay her way through UCLA. She went on to write, produce, and host many TV shows, including *On Cue* for PBS and *Campus Close-Up*. She hosted *Today's Business* on CNBC. She wrote for several sitcoms—*The Wonders Years*, *Golden Girls*, and was head writer for *Thirteen East*. At NBC she won a comedy writing award for the variety special *TV or Not TV*. She received the Best Feature Animation Screenplay Award for *The Secret Island of Tortuga*.

After achieving success as a screenwriter, she turned her attention to children's books, and authored *The King of Skittledeedoo*, which led to the Rust Foundation for Literacy, motivating children through its "Royal Readers" and "Create-a-Book" programs.

As a literacy advocate and children's author, Patricia travels the world presenting her various creative workshops to adults, schools and youth groups. For more information about the Rust Foundation, visit www.PowerFor Kids. com.

51 Not Even a Bullet In His Brain Could Stop Him

by Patricia Rust
for her father, William Evans Rust, Jr.

My father let me shave him when I was little. He would sing, "There is nothing as lovely as a tree," and then he would blot blood from the nicks, and patch my botched shaving job while he spelled out the words for me, his bright eyes dazzling me all the while. I thought he must be the greatest man in the world.

"Lovely, L-O-V-E-L-Y—it has the word 'love' in it. Now it's your turn to spell both words," he would say. He never chastised me, but instead focused on the spelling lesson. I loved him for not making me feel like the spazzy, scrawny (but pretty) kid that I was. He treated me like a princess and called me one, too. At school I became a champion speller!

I remember him best as the tallest man I had ever seen, with black, wavy hair and vivid blue eyes. They spoke of a certain sweetness I had never seen in anyone else's eyes. His smile was sensual and engaging to others, and was as sweet as his eyes, which conveyed only positive messages. When he spoke, his voice was as soothing as honey. This rare combination of sweetness and gentleness allowed him to be, for me, the perfect father and teacher. I couldn't wait to see him each day and, while I adored my mother equally, she was always available to me, but I had to *wait* to see my dad.

My father had a commanding will in this magnificent, God-given package that could put Sean Connery to shame, not only in looks, but in his single raised eyebrow that spoke legions. When that eyebrow went up, I went out! My mother called my father stubborn, but I called him assertive. He would spend hours on end teaching me to read. I recall vividly sitting in his lap while he read *Life Magazine*, spelling Mohammed Ali and Cassius Clay for me. I asked about the bloodied, bruised boxer's eyes, and my father explained the sport of boxing with these words: "Why anyone would want to punch anyone in the face is beyond me. The numbskulls." Numbskull was one of my favorite words he used. It made me laugh.

My father would often entertain us with his jazz clarinet, Jimmy Durante impressions, and reading aloud for hours. He played all the characters. He could imitate Buddy Hackett (to his face) and JFK, and his voice helped me learn to read and write. By kindergarten I could spell and read many things. My second favorite word was "Mississippi" because it was fun to spell. My real favorite word was "lovely."

I lost my father a few months ago, but I do not think of him as dead. He is very much alive in me despite what science tells us. I see his face in flowers and clouds, and while doing ordinary and extraordinary things in my life. I hear his soft voice prodding and encouraging. I feel the pride he had for me, and truly hope I deserve it. I feel him watching over my mother as her guardian angel. I recognize him best when a songbird sings at dawn and hops right into the house as though it lived here, too. I embrace the notion that a soul exists and these souls stay connected even if dimensions change.

My father loved Hawaii because he said, "Here I can live forever." That's where his soul now resides with my mother, who knows he's there. She paints flowers for him daily—the same flowers she had brought to the hospital to cheer him and spread the spirit of aloha.

I have always liked reading biographies because I love to understand what makes people tick. Just after losing someone, it's hard to think of him or her as a biography when the pain of loss still cuts like sharpened shears. The reality of missing the physical presence of the lost one is overwhelming. So forgive me this indulgence, and know that these words come from the heart and are written to inspire others with snippets of a life that made a difference. No one really ever dies. They just change dimensions. Or so goes my hope.

I celebrate that I had my father for so many wonderful, happy, sometimes struggling, sometimes yearning years. Life should never be easy. It should challenge us and make us grow. It should be fraught with peril and doubt and hope and fear, and we should learn as we go. We need to celebrate its tiny victories as much as we celebrate its big ones. We must never master it, because then we would lose the challenge and the goal. There is always more to shoot for, like learning to produce the scent of roses by just thinking of it. There is another language to learn, a new country to explore, a new child to be tended, and our selves to be discovered.

When I lost my dad, I found myself. I found out who I am, what I am made of, and why life is the platinum of metals, the diamond of stones, and the spice of the Spice Wars. He put ingredients into my upbringing that allowed me to make decisions and mistakes (and lots of them) for myself. He never judged, only encouraged me to probe, push, and move forward. He said not moving forward was moving backward.

My father was an elegant man—poised, dignified, and funny beyond measure. He always struck me as a movie star, and when he stood talking and laughing with Jimmy Stewart, it never occurred to me that my father was anything but one. He was handsome and debonair, and I seem to recall my grandfathers were that way, too. Why did our whole society cave in to the wearing of *sweats*? How can anyone hope to carve an image into the hearts of others when they look like something in need of washing?

He always looked his best. My mother, too. I never saw a hair roller or cold cream on her. I saw dashing suits and sparkling gems, and stockings so sheer that they glistened under my mother's party dresses. My parents were not "just having fun" in their outfits, they were raising awareness, raising funds, and doing good for others on a regular basis.

My father would knock on someone's door and say, "This neighborhood needs a library right here. Would you be willing to see that vision through?" And people would say yes. I have great faith in people and don't believe we are seeing real people in real ways anymore. We see freaks, the ones who fell through the cracks. Instead of focusing on the cracks, we focus on the crackheads. My father thought that each and everyone of us could, should, and would make a difference if we just tried. He did not emphasize the success nor the outcome—the emphasis was always on the effort. As a child, I believed my father would someday be President of our country.

Toward the end of his life, my childhood impressions of him were corrected. Now that I know the reality of my father's story, I know why he wasn't a beloved President. I know why he lived the life he did as best as he could with the tools he had been given.

On some level, he must have known his final days were upon him as he shared stories of his own grandparents and parents. He talked of the first girl he kissed under a grand piano, and the love at first sight he experienced with my mother. He moved 3,000 miles to be with her *the next day*. It's strange and eerie to learn about a parent at the end of his life, but it's also lovely to listen and learn what you can from those willing to share.

My father, William Evans Rust, Jr., had wanted to be a career military officer, yet he didn't believe in war. This was a strange revelation to me. He believed in keeping the ideas flowing and the communication going...just so that there was dialogue and movement, and action toward a resolution.

My father taught me how to have a friend and be a friend, with wisdom, brilliance, and a wit that made him bigger than life. Even after his passing, people I had never met knocked on the door and said, "I loved your father more than anyone I have ever met. He made me feel special."

In the last year of his life he was "incarcerated" in the hospital where the staff called him "Cool Hand Bill." He was hooked up to a beeper so that if he tried to make a break for it, it would sound an alarm. He would call my mother and beg, "Honey, come get me. I don't need to be here. My mind is fine."

But he had a bullet in his brain that had been playing tiddlywinks in there since WWII...WE JUST NEVER KNEW IT! When he graduated summa cum laude with a Phi Beta Kappa key, he pulled off his cap and gown, got on the bus to Officer's Training School, then into Special Operations and desert training headed for George Patton's Army in North Africa. He served for eight years until a German bullet put an end to his military career.

His injury went undiagnosed for a lifetime. He was once an athlete and dancer, but the bullet affected the coordination center of his brain. Although this resulted in many injuries from falls due to poor balance, it never broke his spirit. In his Beverly Hills Veterans of Foreign Wars hat, he allowed me to let go of his wheelchair as I headed him straight down from the top of the hill to the ocean. He would then throw up his arms and shout, "Whee!" This is my favorite photo of him with a caption saying, "Live Life Large!"

At the end I shaved Dad just as though I were still his little girl again. My life is better knowing he is there in some version of love and light that dances on my shoulders.

Let's embrace the magic that is joy and life itself. That is the best way to pay tribute to those who have left their indelible marks on our lives.

Lovely is *still* my favorite word.

MARIANN AALDA, C.Ht.

Mariann Aalda can be reached at www.aaldaanswers.com. For biographical information, see page 23.

52 Team "Momma"
(Everything I ever needed to know about fair play, I learned in Little League)

by Mariann Aalda

What's up with all the biting, kicking and spitting that we're seeing so much of in professional sports these days? In a word—testosterone.

That same "jock fuel" that is such an asset to a basketball player when he's on the court, for example, can be a real liability on the freeway when somebody cuts him off in traffic. The same ego that puffs up and pushes him to play to win doesn't conveniently deflate for the sake of others' (not even the coach's) convenience.

Sexist? No. Female biochemistry includes testosterone and it affects us the same way. But estrogen balances us out, soothes the psyche while it softens the epidermis, and also acts as a healing balm for the frayed nerves and bruised egos of the men in our lives.

To take advantage of this quirk of nature, I'd like to advocate the position of "Team Mom" being added to the roster of **every professional sports team (NBA, NFL, etc)**. With her Little League training, she could run a Team Mom intervention program whenever things got a little, well..."test-y." With her TLC and a couple of phone calls, she could even avert catastrophe. Here's how it might work:

PHONE CALL #1

PLAYER: Momma! He's pickin' on me again.

T-MOM: Who, baby?

PLAYER: The coach.

T-MOM: What exactly is he doing, sweetheart?

PLAYER: He's yelling at me and callin' me names in front of the guys.

T-MOM: Honey, that's just his way of motivating you.

PLAYER: But it's *embarrassing* and hurts my feelings, and makes me mad enough to *choke* him!

T-MOM: No hitting, no kicking, no spitting... and *definitely* no choking!

PLAYER: (Contrite) Yes, ma'am.

T-MOM: (Sigh) Okay, what do you want me to do? You want me to talk to him for you?

PLAYER: Would you, Momma? (Mood brightens) That would be great!

T-MOM: No problem...Oh, this may be wishful thinking, but if you fellas make it to the play-offs, I want a championship ring, too, you hear!

PLAYER: Yes, ma'am.

T-MOM: Size six.

PHONE CALL # 2

T-MOM: Hello, Coach? Your best player tells me you two haven't been getting along well lately.

COACH: Oh, Momma, you know I only ride him so hard because he's so damned talented!

T-MOM: *What* did you say!?!

COACH: Sorry...*darned* talented.

T-MOM: Much better.

COACH: Well, he knows how talented he is too, so sometimes he gets lazy at practice and starts goofing off.

T-MOM: How?

COACH: Typical stuff...cracking jokes, not hustling.

T-MOM: But Coach, it's only practice...doesn't he always come through for the games?

COACH: No question. But he's setting a bad example for the other players who don't have his ability. And these guys *need to work hard at practice* to be at peak performance for the game.

T-MOM: Well, I still don't think yelling and name-calling is the answer. Remember, you're the oldest, so you should be setting the example of good sportsmanship.

COACH: (Thoughtfully) Hmmm...

T-MOM: Mmmm...Hmmm. (long pause) Coach, are you sure you're not yelling at him because he's younger and makes so much more money?

COACH: (Silence)

T-MOM: Come on now, isn't it possible that you could be just a little bit...*jealous?*

COACH: Well...not consciously.

T-MOM: That's okay, darlin'. We all get a little envious sometimes. Wouldn't be human if we didn't.

COACH: But *you* don't.

T-MOM: As long as I don't turn on *Entertainment Tonight* and see that little Jada Pinkett with that *fine* Will Smith, I don't!

COACH: Oh, Momma! He's young enough to be your...

T-MOM: (Interrupting) Only makes it worse...just reminds me that *my* playing days are over.

COACH: Got the picture.

T-MOM: Knew you would. The front office didn't hire you just because you look so handsome on television.

COACH: Oh, Momma, now you've got me blushing.

T-MOM: Feels good, too, doesn't it? Always feels good when somebody says nice things about you to your face. Makes you want to run right out to the court and shoot a three-pointer, doesn't it?

COACH: (Pause) I got it now.

T-MOM: Oh, Coach, just one more thing. Some of the fellas have been tellin' me that they're gettin' a little tired of the Ring Dings. So for next week's half-time snack...think I should switch to Twinkies?

Reflecting on this scenario is a reminder that, as women, we all have "Team Mom" potential, whether it's on the basketball court, in the board room, or in the bedroom. And while we may not have the strength to restrain conflict, we *do* have a power we can exercise to *resolve* it.

CONTRIBUTORS

Mariann Aalda, C.Ht. *19, 275*
Glenn Ackerman *143*
Don Albrecht *239*
John Alston *99*
Beverly Bacon *69*
Frank Becker *219*
Gray Berg, D.D.S. *113*
Victoria Bullis *253*
Tad Callister *139*
Bernadene Coleman *227*
William Dahlberg, D.D.S. *223*
William Derringer *207*
John H. Dilkes *11*
Harris Done, D.D.S. *155*
John Ernst *189*
Michael Fenlon, M.D. *63*
Devra Hill, Ph.D. *261*
Walter Hofmann, M.D. *25*
James F. Holt *47*
Ed Hibler, Ed.D. *179, 195*
Rex Ingraham, D.D.S. *105*
Judith Jefferies *201*
Janie Lee *119*

Roger Leir, D.P.M. *93*
Lael Littke *77*
Eugene Manusov, D.D.S. *83*
Sol Marshall *249*
Wink Martindale *73*
Pilar McRae *185*
Val Middlebrook *35*
Susan Moss *243*
Esther Pearlman *213*
Margaret Rector *235*
Audrey Reed, D.S.S. *265*
Ellen Reid *59*
Patricia Rust *269*
Bernice Schachter *41*
Ray Schnieders *167*
Margaret Schumacher *15*
Astronaut Rick Searfoss *149*
(Three-time NASA Shuttle Commander)
Joyce Spizer *53*
Elizabeth Thompson *135*
Lisa Todd *31*
Dottie Walters *123*
Ernie Weckbaugh *109, 159, 175*
Patty Weckbaugh *131, 159, 163*
Bob West, D.D.S. *87*

Published by Best-Seller Books and Casa Graphics, Inc., Burbank, CA 91504 • To order books, email: casag@wgn.net

Afterwords

"...these are stories that make the heart want to sing, the soul want to dance."

—Ruth Klein, President of
the Time Marketing Source,
author of *Where Did the Time Go?* and
Manage Your Time/Market Your Business

"...may you reap millions with this one! You've earned it."

—Al Winnikoff,
co-author of *Millionaire*

"...what I like throughout this book is the triumph of the human spirit!"

—Lloyd Wright, author of
Triumph Over Hepatitis C

"...has all the winning ingredients of a steady seller for years to come."

—Jim Blasingame, host of
The Small Business Advocate
and author of *Small Business
Is Like a Bunch of Bananas*

"...an uplifting bit of medicine if you get down at times."

—Harold Cottle, M.D., Altoona, PA

"...makes for a tasty reading snack any time of the day."

—Dave Balch, author of *Cancer for Two*